From AI To ET

by

Ian Beardsley

ISBN: 978-1-365-07860-6

Ian Beardsley

From AI To ET

From AI To ET

A Great Mystery Is Before Us

Explore The Enigma of Artificial Intelligence!

The main components of AI are made of silicon (Si) doped with.
Phosphorus (P) and Boron (B).
Si=28.09, P=30.97, B=10.81
How many numbers averaged?: 2
1 enter number: 10.81
2 enter number: 30.97
The sum of your numbers is: 41.78
The arithmetic mean is: 20.89
We find the harmonic and geometric means between a and b.
enter a: 30.97
enter b: 10.81
harmonic mean is 16.03
geometric mean is 18.30
If you chose phosphorus and boron for a and b,...
would you like me to divide the results by silicon? 1=yes, 0=no: 1
harmonic/Si is: 0.57
geometric/Si is: 0.65
Would you like me to take the arithmetic mean between these results? 1
The arithmetic mean of the harmonic and geometric means is: 0.61
That is the golden ratio conjugate.
This means that:

$$\frac{(\sqrt{PB})(P+B)+2PB}{2(P+B)(Si)} = phi = 0.6$$

We looked at silicon doped with phosphorus and boron,...
But, Gallium (Ga) and Arsenic (As) can be used as doping agents,..
As well, we can use Germanium (Ge) in place of Silicon (Si),...
for the semimetal.
Germanium = 72.61, Gallium = 69.72, Arsenic = 74.92.
Give me a the doping agent Ga: 69.72
Give me b the doping agent As: 74.92
The harmonic mean is 72.23
The geometric mean is 72.27
Notice the hamonic/geometric for Ga and As, is close to Germanium (Ge)
Germanium was the first generation semiconductor.
This would suggest logic gates using these doping agents,...
Should be doping Germanium for first generation robots,
This says:

$$sqrt((Ga)(As)) \sim Ge$$

```
Si=28.09, P=30.97,   B=10.81
Ge=72.61, Ga=69.72, As=74.92
Let us find the geometric mean between P and B:
Enter P: 30.97
Enter B: 10.81
Let us find the geometric mean between Ga and As:
Enter Ga: 69.72
Enter As: 74.92
geometric for P and B = 18.30
geometric for Ga and As = 72.27
Let us now add sqrt(Ga*As) to sqrt(P*B)
Then divide the result by 2 times Si
We divide by double Si, because we have added the mean of,...
two doping agents, to the mean of another two doping agents.
sqrt(Ga*As)+sqrt(PB) = 90.57
Input Si and I will divide 2Si into the above sum: 28.09
(sqrt(Ga*As)+sqrt(PB))/2Si =: 1.61
This is the golden ratio (PHI) which equals 1.6
We have therefore discovered:

    sqrt(Ga*As)+sqrt(PB)
    ------------------------  =  PHI
           2(Si)
```

```
   (sqrt(PB))(P+B))+2PB
   ----------------------    = phi
        2(P+B)(Si)
```

```
(sqrt(PB))(P+B)=764.4486
2(PB)=669.5714
sqrt(764,4486)=27.64866
sqrt(669.5714)=25.876
(27.64866+25.876)/2 = 26.76233
This is approximately equal to aluminum (Al)
Al=26.98
```

```
2(P+B)(Si)=2,347.2004
sqrt(2,347.2004)=48.4479
This is approximately equal to titanium (Ti)
Ti=47.88
```

This says a second generation robot,...
should have a skeleton composed of,…

titanium-aluminum alloy

```
Phosporus, P = 30.97
    Boron, B = 10.81

 Silicon, Si = 28.09

geometric mean = sqrt(PB)
harmonic mean = 2PB/(P+B)

int mean=0
while mean!=2
{
mean=mean+1
print Si=Si+char, Si
print mean + char, mean
}

out[1] mean 1 + mean 2
out[2] Si + Si

out[2] proportional to out[1]
constant of proportionality is phi=0.6=golden ratio conjugate

that means: (Si+Si)(phi)=(mean 1)+(mean 2)
or, 2Si(phi)=sqrt(PB) + 2PB/(P+B)
```

This is significant because it means silicon doped
with phosphorus
and boron has the golden ratio conjugate in its means.
Silicon doped with phosphorus and boron make diodes and transistors:
So artificial intelligence has phi in it, like life does.

```
enter mean: sqrt(PB)
enter silicon: Si
mean + sqrt(PB)
silicon + Si

2(Si)phi = mean1 + mean2
enter mean 1: sqrt(PB)
enter mean 2: 2PB/(P+B)
enter silicon: Si
enter phi: phi
mean + sqrt(PB)
silicon + Si




2(Si)(phi) = sqrt(PB) + 2PB/(P+B)
The veins of AI should be copper. The protective skin
any insulator, but the simplest is plastic
which is, C2H4
C=12.01 and H = 1.01
C2 = 2(12.01)=24.02 and H4=4.04
C2+H4=(24.02+4.04)=28.06~Si=28.09
This says a robots veins are about equal to
A robot's silicon components.
logout

[Process completed]
```

```c
#include <stdio.h>
#include <math.h>
int main (void)
{
printf("\n");
printf("Explore The Enigma of Artificial Intelligence!\n");
printf("\n");
printf("The main components of AI are made of silicon (Si) doped with.
\n");
printf("Phosphorus (P) and Boron (B).\n");
printf("Si=28.09, P=30.97, B=10.81\n");
int n;
int i;
do
{
printf ("How many numbers averaged?: ");
scanf("%d", &n);
}
while (n<0);

float num[n],sum=0.0,average;
for (i=1; i<=n; i++)
{
printf("%i enter number: ", i);
scanf("%f", &num[n]);
sum+=num[n];
average=sum/n;
}
printf("The sum of your numbers is: %.2f\n", sum);
printf("The arithmetic mean is: %.2f\n", average);

float a, b,total, product, harmonic, geometric, answer;
printf("We find the harmonic and geometric means between a and b.\n");
printf("enter a: ");
scanf("%f", &a);
printf("enter b: ");
scanf("%f", &b);
product=2*a*b;
total=a+b;
harmonic=product/total;
geometric=sqrt(a*b);
printf("harmonic mean is %.2f\n", harmonic);
printf("geometric mean is %.2f\n",geometric);
printf("If you chose phosphorus and boron for a and b,...\n");
printf("would you like me to divide the results by silicon? 1=yes,
0=no: ");
scanf("%f", &answer);
```

```
if (answer==1)
{
printf("harmonic/Si is: %.2f \n",harmonic/28.09);
printf("geometric/Si is: %.2f\n", geometric/28.09);
printf("Would you like me to take the arithmetic mean between these
results? ");
scanf("%f", &answer);
if (answer==1)
{
printf("The arithmetic mean of the harmonic and geometric means is:
0.61\n");
printf("That is the golden ratio conjugate.\n");
}
printf("This means that:\n");
printf("\n");
printf("\n");
printf("    (sqrt(PB))(P+B)+2PB\n");
printf("    ----------------------  =  phi=0.6\n");
printf("        2(P+B)(Si)");
printf("\n");
printf("\n");
printf("closing sesssion\n");


    float a, b, product, sum, geometrics, harmonic;
    printf("We looked at silicon doped with phosphorus and boron,...
\n");
    printf("But, Gallium (Ga) and Arsenic (As) can be used as doping
agents,..\n");
    printf("As well, we can use Germanium (Ge) in place of Silicon
(Si),...\n");
    printf("for the semimetal.\n");
    printf("Germanium = 72.61, Gallium = 69.72, Arsenic = 74.92.\n");
    printf("Give me a the doping agent Ga: ");
    scanf("%f", &a);
    printf("Give me b the doping agent As: ");
    scanf("%f", &b);
    product=2*a*b;
    sum=a+b;
    geometrics=sqrt(a*b);
    harmonic=product/sum;
    printf("The harmonic mean is %.2f\n", harmonic);
    printf("The geometric mean is %.2f\n", geometrics);
    printf("Notice the hamonic/geometric for Ga and As, is close to
Germanium (Ge)\n");
    printf("Germanium was the first generation semiconductor.\n");
```

```
    printf("This would suggest logic gates using these doping
agents,...\n");
    printf("Should be doping Germanium for first generation robots,
\n");
    printf("This says:\n");
    printf("\n");
    printf("    sqrt((Ga)(As))~Ge\n");
    printf("\n");
    printf("\n");

    float P, B, Ga=0.0, As=0.0, geo, geometric, Si, doubled, twicesi;
    printf("Si=28.09, P=30.97,  B=10.81\n");
    printf("Ge=72.61, Ga=69.72, As=74.92\n");
    printf("Let us find the geometric mean between P and B:\n");
    printf("Enter P: ");
    scanf("%f", &P);
    printf("Enter B: ");
    scanf("%f", &B);
    geo=sqrt(P*B);
    printf("Let us find the geometric mean between Ga and As:\n");
    printf("Enter Ga: ");
    scanf("%f", &Ga);
    printf("Enter As: ");
    scanf("%f", &As);
    geometric=sqrt(Ga*As);
    printf("geometric for P and B = %.2f\n", geo);
    printf("geometric for Ga and As = %.2f\n", geometric);
    printf("Let us now add sqrt(Ga*As) to sqrt(P*B)\n");
    printf("Then divide the result by 2 times Si\n");
    printf("We divide by double Si, because we have added the mean
of,...\n");
    printf("two doping agents, to the mean of another two doping
agents.\n");
    printf("sqrt(Ga*As)+sqrt(PB) = %.2f\n", geo + geometric);
    printf("Input Si and I will divide 2Si into the above sum: ");
    scanf("%f", &Si);
    twicesi=2*Si;
    doubled=geo+geometric;
    printf("(sqrt(Ga*As)+sqrt(PB))/2Si =: %.2f\n", doubled/twicesi);
    printf("This is the golden ratio (PHI) which equals 1.6\n");
    printf("We have therefore discovered:\n");
    printf("\n");
    printf("    sqrt(Ga*As)+sqrt(PB)\n");
    printf("    ------------------------  =  PHI\n");
    printf("            2(Si)              ");
    printf("\n");
    printf("\n");
```

```
printf("\n");
printf("\n");
printf("   (sqrt(PB))(P+B))+2PB\n");
printf("   --------------------   = phi\n");
printf("          2(P+B)(Si)          ");
printf("\n");
printf("\n");
printf("(sqrt(PB))(P+B)=764.4486\n");
printf("2(PB)=669.5714\n");
printf("sqrt(764,4486)=27.64866\n");
printf("sqrt(669.5714)=25.876\n");
printf("(27.64866+25.876)/2 = 26.76233\n");
printf("This is approximately equal to aluminum (Al)\n");
printf("Al=26.98");
printf("\n");
printf("\n");
printf("2(P+B)(Si)=2,347.2004\n");
printf("sqrt(2,347.2004)=48.4479\n");
printf("This is approximately equal to titanium (Ti)\n");
printf("Ti=47.88\n");
printf("\n");
printf("This says a second generation robot,...\n");
printf("should have a skeleton composed of,...\n");
printf("titanium-aluminum alloy\n");
printf("\n");

printf("\n");
printf("Phosporus, P = 30.97\n");
printf("    Boron, B = 10.81\n");
printf("\n");
printf(" Silicon, Si = 28.09\n");
printf("\n");
printf("geometric mean = sqrt(PB)\n");
printf("harmonic mean = 2PB/(P+B)\n");
printf("\n");
printf("int mean=0\n");
printf("while mean!=2\n");
printf("{\n");
printf("mean=mean+1\n");
printf("print Si=Si+char, Si\n");
printf("print mean + char, mean\n");
printf("}\n");
printf("\n");
printf("out[1] mean 1 + mean 2\n");
printf("out[2] Si + Si\n");
```

```
    printf("\n");
    printf("out[2] proportional to out[1]");
    printf("\n");
    printf("constant of proportionality is phi=0.6=golden ratio
conjugate");
    printf("\n");
    printf("\n");
    printf("that means: (Si+Si)(phi)=(mean 1)+(mean 2)");
    printf("\n");
    printf("or, 2Si(phi)=sqrt(PB) + 2PB/(P+B)");
    printf("\n");
    printf("\n");
    printf("This is significant because it means silicon doped\n");
    printf("with phosphorus\n");
    printf("and boron has the golden ratio conjugate in its means.
\n");
    printf("Silicon doped with phosphorus and boron make diodes and
transistors:\n");
    printf("So artifical intelligence has phi in it, like life does.
\n");
    printf("\n");



    char a1[15]; char b1[15];


        printf("enter mean: ");
        scanf("%s", a1);
        printf("enter silicon: ");
        scanf("%s", b1);

        printf("mean + %s\n", a1);
        printf("silicon + %s\n", b1);
        printf("\n");
        printf("2(%s)phi = mean1 + mean2", b1);
        printf("\n");



{
    int mean = 1;
    char a[15]; char b[15]; char c[15]; char d[15];
    while (mean!=2)
    {
        mean=mean+1;
```

```c
        printf("enter mean 1: ");
        scanf("%s", a);
        printf("enter mean 2: ");
        scanf("%s", b);
        printf("enter silicon: ");
        scanf("%s", c);
        printf("enter phi: ");
        scanf("%s", d);

        printf("mean + %s\n", a);
        printf("silicon + %s\n", c);
        printf("\n");
        printf("2(%s)(%s) = %s + %s",c, d, a, b);
        printf("\n");
    }

printf("The veins of AI should be copper. The protective skin\n");
printf("any insulator, but the simplest is plastic\n");
printf("which is, C2H4\n");
printf("C=12.01 and H = 1.01\n");
printf("C2 = 2(12.01)=24.02 and H4=4.04\n");
printf("C2+H4=(24.02+4.04)=28.06~Si=28.09\n");
printf("This says a robots veins are about equal to\n");
printf("A robot's silicon components.\n");
}
}
}
```

```
jharvard@appliance (~): cd Dropbox
jharvard@appliance (~/Dropbox): make input
clang -ggdb3 -O0 -std=c99 -Wall -Werror   input.c  -lcs50 -lm -o input
jharvard@appliance (~/Dropbox): ./input
```

Sierra Waters
The Brain
Enter Last Name: Waters
Enter First Name: Sierra
Enter Name: Brain
Enter Definite Article: The
Waters, Sierra: She was handed the newly discovered document in 2042.
Brain, The: He designed hyperdrive in 2044.
Between 2042 and 2044 is 2043.

If we use alphacentauri as the key to our model,
for modeling the future, then our task has been reduced,
through the work I have done, to quite a simple one.
growthrate=k=0.0621, objective=log 100/log e = 4.6 achievements,
Tzero=1969 when we landed on the moon, which at 2009 is 0.552=.0.12(4.6)
1/0.55 = 1.8=9/5 = R/r = Au/Ag, putting us in the age of gold:silver
Our equation is then, Time=(Object Achieved)/(Achievements/year)

How many simulations would you like to run (10 max)? 2
What is percent development towards objective(0-100)? 100
What is the starting point (year:enter 1969) ?1969
Time to object=74.165016 years.
That is the year: 2043.165039
What is percent development towards objective(0-100)? 7.4
What is the starting point (year:enter 1969) ?1969
Time to object=32.233292 years.
That is the year: 2001.233276

If you chose tzero as moon landing (1969), then you found
obect acheived 2043 between Sierra Waters and The Brain.
That time being reached in 74 years after time zero.
If you ran a second simulation again with t zero at 1969, and
ran the program for the 74 years to hyperdrive reduced by
a factor of ten (that is input 7.4 percent development.)
Then, you found object achieved in 2001, the year of Kubrick's
Starchild

jharvard@appliance (~/Dropbox):
```
```

```c
#include <stdio.h>
#include <math.h>
int main (void)
{
printf("\n");
char s[15], w[15], t[5], b[10];
printf("Sierra Waters\n");
printf("The Brain\n");
printf("Enter Last Name: ");
scanf("%s", w);
printf("Enter First Name: ");
scanf("%s", s);
printf("Enter Name: ");
scanf("%s", b);
printf("Enter Definite Article: ");
scanf("%s", t);
printf("%s, %s: She was handed the newly discovered document in
2042.\n", w, s);
printf("%s, %s: He designed hyperdrive in 2044.\n", b, t);
printf("Between 2042 and 2044 is 2043.\n");
printf("\n");
printf("\n");
float object, Tzero, T, time, L;
int n;
printf("If we use alphacentauri as the key to our model,\n");
printf("for modeling the future, then our task has been reduced,\n");
printf("through the work I have done, to quite a simple one.\n");
printf("growthrate=k=0.0621, objective=log 100/log e = 4.6
achievements,\n");
printf("Tzero=1969 when we landed on the moon, which at 2009 is
0.552=.0.12(4.6)\n");
printf("1/0.55 = 1.8=9/5 = R/r = Au/Ag, putting us in the age of
gold:silver\n");
printf("Our equation is then, Time=(Object Achieved)/(Achievements/
year)\n");
printf("\n");

do
{
printf("How many simulations would you like to run (10 max)? ");
scanf("%d", &n);
}
while (n>10 && n<=0);
for (int i=1; i<=n; i++)
{
do
{
```

```
printf("What is percent development towards objective(0-100)? ");
scanf("%f", &object);
}
while (n<0 && n>100);
printf("What is the starting point (year:enter 1969) ?");
scanf("%f", &Tzero);
L= ((log10 (object))/((log10 (2.718)))));
T=L/(0.0621);
time= Tzero+T;
printf("Time to object=%f years.\n", T);
printf("That is the year: %f\n", time);
}
printf("\n");
printf("If you chose tzero as moon landing (1969), then you found\n");
printf("obect acheived 2043 between Sierra Waters and The Brain.\n");
printf("That time being reached in 74 years after time zero.\n");
printf("If you ran a second simulation again with t zero at 1969, and
\n");
printf("ran the program for the 74 years to hyperdrive reduced by\n");
printf("a factor of ten (that is input 7.4 percent development.)\n");
printf("Then, you found object achieved in 2001, the year of Kubrick's
\n");
printf("Starchild\n");
printf("\n");
}
```

Star System: Alpha Centauri
Spectral Class: Same As The Sun
Proximity: Nearest Star System
Value For Projecting Human Trajectory: Ideal

The probability of landing at four light years from earth at Alpha Centauri in 10 random leaps of one light year each (to left or right) is given by the equation of a random walk:

{ W }_{ n }({ n }_{ 1 })=\frac { N! }{ { n }_{ 1 }!{ n }_{ 2 }! } { p }^{ n1 }{ q }^{ n2 }\\
N={ n }_{ 1 }+{ n }_{ 2 }\\ q+p=1

$$W_n(n_1) = \frac{N!}{n_1! n_2!} p^{n1} q^{n2}$$

$$N = n_1 + n_2$$

$$q + p = 1$$

To land at plus four we must jump 3 to the left, 7 to the right (n1=3, n2 = 7: 7+3=10):

Using our equation:

$$\frac{(10!)}{(7!)(3!)}\left(\frac{1}{2}\right)^7\left(\frac{1}{2}\right)^3 = \frac{3628800}{(5040)(6)}\frac{1}{128}\frac{1}{8} = \frac{120}{1024} = \frac{15}{128} = 0.1171875 \approx 12\%$$

We would be, by this reasoning 12% along in the development towards hyperdrive.

Having calculated that we are 12% along in developing the hyperdrive, we can use the equation for natural growth to estimate when we will have hyperdrive. It is of the form:

$$x(t) = x_0 e^{kt}$$

t is time and k is a growth rate constant which we must determine to solve the equation. In 1969 Neil Armstrong became the first man to walk on the moon. In 2009 the European Space Agency launched the Herschel and Planck telescopes that will see back to near the beginning of the universe. 2009-1969 is 40 years. This allows us to write:

$$12\% = e^{k(40)}$$

$$\log 12 = 40k \log 2.718$$

$$0.026979531 = 0.4342 \, k$$

$$k = 0.0621$$

We now can write:

$$x(t) = e^{(0.0621)t}$$

$$100\% = e^{(0.0621)t}$$

$$\log 100 = (0.0621) \, t \log e$$

$$t = 74 \text{ years}$$

$$1969 + 74 \text{ years} = 2043$$

Our reasoning would indicate that we will have hyperdrive in the year 2043.

Study summary:

1. We have a 70% chance of developing hyperdrive without destroying ourselves first.
2. We are 12% along the way in development of hyperdrive.
3. We will have hyperdrive in the year 2043, plus or minus.

Sierra Waters was handed the newly discovered document in 2042.

modelfuture

When you write a program that gets the same results as you did by
hand, you know you have not made an error. This program, designed to
project the future, is more sophisticated than the work I did by hand
in the Levinson story, because we can now adjust the probabilities, p
and q, and use any destination star we wish. Here is the program,
which I call "model future" (modelfuture.c). I have already written
programs, bioplanet, model planet and model ocean. Have combined them
in one work called star system. They will be presented at the end of
this paper.

For now, here is the code in C for model future, and a sample run that
shows the calculations in the Levinson story, are accurate.

```c
#include <stdio.h>
#include <math.h>
int main (void)
{
printf("\n");
int N, r;
double u, v, y, z;
double t,loga, ratio;
int n1, n2;
char name[15];
float W,fact=1,fact2=1,fact3=1,a,g,rate,T,T1;
double x,W2;
printf("(p^n1)(q^n2)[W=N!/(n1!)(n2!)]");
printf("\n");
printf("x=e^(c*t)");
printf("\n");
printf("W is the probability of landing on the star in N jumps.\n");
printf("N=n1+n2, n1=number of one light year jumps left,\n");
printf("n2=number of one light year jumps right.\n");
printf("What is 1, the nearest whole number of light years to the
star, and\n");
printf("2, what is the star's name?\n");
printf("Enter 1: ");
scanf("%i", &r);
printf("Enter 2: ");
scanf("%s", name);
printf("Star name: %s\n", name);
printf("Distance: %i\n", r);
printf("What is n1? ");
scanf("%i", &n1);
printf("What is n2? ");
scanf("%i", &n2);
printf("Since N=n1+n2, N=%i\n", n1+n2);
N=n1+n2;
printf("What is the probability, p(u), of jumping to the left? ");
scanf("%lf", &u);
printf("What is the probability, p(v), of jumpint to the left? ");
scanf("%lf", &v);
printf("What is the probability, q(y), of jumping to the right? ");
scanf("%lf", &y);
printf("What is the probability, q(z), of jumping to the right? ");
scanf("%lf", &z);
printf("p=u:v");
printf("\n");
printf("q=y:z");
printf("\n");
for (int i=1; i<=N; i++)
```

```c
{
fact = fact*i;
printf("N factorial = %f\n", fact);

a=pow(u/v,n1)*pow(y/z,n2);
}
for (int j=1; j<=n1; j++)
{
fact2 = fact2*j;
printf("n1 factorial = %f\n", fact2);
}
for (int k=1; k<=n2; k++)
{
fact3 = fact3*k;
printf("n2 factorial = %f\n", fact3);

x=2.718*2.718*2.718*2.718*2.718;
g=sqrt(x);
W=a*fact/(fact2*fact3);
printf("W=%f percent\n", W*100);
W2=100*W;
printf("W=%.2f percent rounded to nearest integral\n", round(W2));
}
{
printf("What is t in years, the time over which the growth occurs? ");
scanf("%lf", &t);
loga=log10(round(W*100));
printf("log(W)=%lf\n", loga);
ratio=loga/t;
printf("loga/t=%lf\n", ratio);
rate=ratio/0.4342; //0.4342 = log e//
printf("growthrate constant=%lf\n", rate);
printf("log 100 = 2, log e = 0.4342, therfore\n");
printf("T=2/[(0.4342)(growthrate)]\n");
T=2/((0.4342)*(rate));
printf("T=%.2f years\n", T);
printf("What was the begin year for the period of growth? ");
scanf("%f", &T1);
printf("Object achieved in %.2f\n", T+T1);
}
}
```

```
jharvard@appliance (~): cd Dropbox
jharvard@appliance (~/Dropbox): make modelfuture
clang -ggdb3 -O0 -std=c99 -Wall -Werror   modelfuture.c  -lcs50 -lm -o modelfuture
jharvard@appliance (~/Dropbox): ./modelfuture

(p^n1)(q^n2)[W=N!/(n1!)(n2!)]
x=e^(c*t)
W is the probability of landing on the star in N jumps.
N=n1+n2, n1=number of one light year jumps left,
n2=number of one light year jumps right.
What is 1, the nearest whole number of light years to the star, and
2, what is the star's name?
Enter 1: 4
Enter 2: alphacentauri
Star name: alphacentauri
Distance: 4
What is n1? 3
What is n2? 7
Since N=n1+n2, N=10
What is the probability, p(u), of jumping to the left? 1
What is the probability, p(v), of jumpint to the left? 2
What is the probability, q(y), of jumping to the right? 1
What is the probability, q(z), of jumping to the right? 2
p=u:v
q=y:z
N factorial = 1.000000
N factorial = 2.000000
N factorial = 6.000000
N factorial = 24.000000
N factorial = 120.000000
N factorial = 720.000000
N factorial = 5040.000000
N factorial = 40320.000000
N factorial = 362880.000000
N factorial = 3628800.000000
n1 factorial = 1.000000
n1 factorial = 2.000000
n1 factorial = 6.000000
n2 factorial = 1.000000
W=59062.500000 percent
W=59063.00 percent rounded to nearest integral
n2 factorial = 2.000000
W=29531.250000 percent
W=29531.00 percent rounded to nearest integral
```

n2 factorial = 6.000000
W=9843.750000 percent
W=9844.00 percent rounded to nearest integral
n2 factorial = 24.000000
W=2460.937500 percent
W=2461.00 percent rounded to nearest integral
n2 factorial = 120.000000
W=492.187500 percent
W=492.00 percent rounded to nearest integral
n2 factorial = 720.000000
W=82.031250 percent
W=82.00 percent rounded to nearest integral
n2 factorial = 5040.000000
W=11.718750 percent
W=12.00 percent rounded to nearest integral
What is t in years, the time over which the growth occurs? 40
log(W)=1.079181
loga/t=0.026980
growthrate constant=0.062136
log 100 = 2, log e = 0.4342, therfore
T=2/[(0.4342)(growthrate)]
T=74.13 years
What was the begin year for the period of growth? 1969
Object achieved in 2043.13
jharvard@appliance (~/Dropbox):

Electron Volt: A unit of energy equal to the work done on an electron in accelerating it through a potential of one volt. It is 1.6E10-19 Joules (Google Search Engine)

Volt: Potential energy that will impart on joule of energy per coulomb of charge that passes through it. (Wikipedia)

Coulomb: The charge of 6.242E18 protons or 6.242E18 electrons.

Forward Bias: A diode (silicon) must have 0.7 volts across it to turn it on, 0.3 volts (Germanium). This is called forward voltage. The forward voltage threshold is 0.6 volts.

(0.6 volts)(1.6E-19)=9.6E-20 Joules

This is the energy to turn on a diode, or the threshold of life for artificial intelligence.

Aerobic respiration requires oxygen (O_2) in order to generate ATP. Although carbohydrates, fats, and proteins are consumed as reactants, it is the preferred method of pyruvate breakdown in glycolysis and requires that pyruvate enter the mitochondria in order to be fully oxidized by the Krebs cycle. The products of this process are carbon dioxide and water, but the energy transferred is used to break strong bonds in ADP as the third phosphate group is added to form ATP (adenosine triphosphate), by substrate-level phosphorylation, NADH and FADH2

Simplified reaction:

$C_6H_{12}O_6$ (s) + 6 O_2 (g) → 6 CO_2 (g) + 6 H_2O (l) + heat
ΔG = –2880 kJ per mol of $C_6H_{12}O_6$

(From Wikipedia)

(2,880,000 J)/(6.02E23 C6H12O6) =4.784E-18 J = basic unit of biological life
(4.784E-18 J)/(9.6E-20 J)=49.8~50

This says the basic energy unit of organic, or biological life, is about 50 times greater than the basic energy unit of electronic life, or artificial intelligence.

That is 0.6(50)=30 electron volts = basic unit of energy for biological life.

So, we see the visible spectrum for one photon of light begins where the energy of the photon is 2 "bue" electronic which is 100 "bue" biological and that that photon has a wavelength of 1.0 micrometers.

This is all about vision in a robot or AI.

```
+1.2eV — — — — — |>— — — — — — — — —> out (9.6E-20 J, or 0.6 eV)
                     |
                     |
         — — — — —|>— — —|
                     |
                     |
                     R
                     |
                     |
         — — — — — — — —
```

A photon has to have a minimum energy of 1.2 electron volts to impart to an electron for it to turn on the simplest of logic gates; a one on, one off, OR GATE, for there to be an output of one "bue" (basic unit of energy electronic) , which 9.6E-20 Joules, as I have calculated it.

Use Planck's Equation: $E=h\nu$ where h= 6.626E-34 Joule seconds

ν=2(9.6E-20)/(6.626E-34)=3.067E14 cycles per second

wavelength = lambda = c/ν where c is the speed of light equal to 3E8 m/s

lambda = (3E8)/(3.067E-34) = 9.78E-7 meters

1 micrometer = 1E-6 meters

lambda ~ 1 micrometer (This is where the visible spectrum begins)

So we see the visible spectrum for one photon of light begins where the energy is 2 bue.

Appendices

I am writing a program in C and Python called *Discover*. It searches for hidden nuances in Nature and the Universe. The first program is called *add*. It is based on:

The arithmetic mean is the midpoint, c, between two extremes a, and c:

$$b = \frac{a+c}{2}$$

The harmonic mean is not necessarily the midpoint between two extremes but is the value that occurs most frequently:

$$b = \frac{2ac}{a+c}$$

The geometric mean, b, between a and c, is the side of a square that has the same area as a rectangle with sides a and c:

$$b = \sqrt{ac}$$

The following relationship holds:

$$a : \frac{a+c}{2} :: \frac{2ac}{a+c} : c$$

The Golden Ratio

Let us draw a line and divide it such that the length of that line divided by the larger section is equal to the larger section divided by the smaller section. That ratio is The Golden Ratio, or phi:

$$\frac{a}{b} = \frac{b}{c}$$

$$a = b + c$$

$$c = a - b$$

$$a(a - b) = b^2$$

$$a^2 - ab = b^2$$

$$a^2 - ab - b^2 = 0$$

$$\left(\frac{a}{b}\right)^2 - \frac{a}{b} - 1 = 0$$

$$\left(\frac{a}{b}\right)^2 - \frac{a}{b} = 1$$

$$\left(\frac{a}{b}\right)^2 - \frac{a}{b} + \frac{1}{4} = \frac{5}{4}$$

$$\left(\frac{a}{b} - \frac{1}{2}\right)^2 = \frac{5}{4}$$

$$\frac{a}{b} = \frac{\sqrt{5} + 1}{2} = 1.618...$$

While Loop In Python

count.py

```python
n=int(raw_input('Count to this integer: '))
x=0
if n>0:
  while (x!=n):
    x=x+1
    print(str(x))
else:
    print('Give me a positive integer.')
```

While Loop In C

cuenta.c

```c
#include <stdio.h>
int main(void)
{
int i=0;
int n;
printf("Give me an integer less than 10: ");
scanf("%i", &n);
while (n>0)
{
i=i+1;
n=n-1;
printf("%i\n", i);
}
}
```

For Loop In Python

For Loops in Python and C

cuenta.py

```python
n=int(raw_input("Give me a positive int: "))
for number in range(1, n+1):
    print(str(number))
```

For Loop In C

count.c

```c
#include<stdio.h>
int main (void)
{
int n;
do
{
printf("Count to this integer: ");
scanf("%d", &n);
}
while (n<=0);
for (int i = 1; i<=n; i++)
{
printf("%d\n", i);
}
}
```

Running the For Loop in C (Does same thing as the While Loops)

jharvard@appliance (~): cd Dropbox/descubrir
jharvard@appliance (~/Dropbox/descubrir): ./count
Count to this integer: 5
1
2
3
4
5
jharvard@appliance (~/Dropbox/descubrir):

Appendix 2

jharvard@appliance (~): cd Dropbox
jharvard@appliance (~/Dropbox): ./objective

If we use alphacentauri as the key to our model,
for modeling the future, then our task has been reduced,
through the work I have done, to quite a simple one.
growthrate=k=0.0621, objective=log 100/log e = 4.6 achievements,
Tzero=1969 when we landed on the moon, which at 2009 is 0.552=.0.12(4.6)
1/0.55 = 1.8=9/5 = R/r = Au/Ag, putting us in the age of gold:silver
Our equation is then, Time=(Object Achieved)/(Achievements/year)

How many simulations would you like to run (10 max)? 8
What is percent develpment towards objective(0-100)? 15
What is the starting point (year:enter 1969) ?1969
Time to object=43.612415 years.
That is the year: 2012.612427

What is percent develpment towards objective(0-100)? 30
What is the starting point (year:enter 1969) ?1969
Time to object=54.775364 years.
That is the year: 2023.775391

What is percent develpment towards objective(0-100)? 45
What is the starting point (year:enter 1969) ?1969
Time to object=61.305267 years.
That is the year: 2030.305298

What is percent develpment towards objective(0-100)? 60
What is the starting point (year:enter 1969) ?1969
Time to object=65.938309 years.
That is the year: 2034.938354

What is percent develpment towards objective(0-100)? 75
What is the starting point (year:enter 1969) ?1969
Time to object=69.531982 years.
That is the year: 2038.531982

What is percent develpment towards objective(0-100)? 90
What is the starting point (year:enter 1969) ?1969
Time to object=72.468216 years.
That is the year: 2041.468262

What is percent develpment towards objective(0-100)? 100
What is the starting point (year:enter 1969) ?1969

Time to object=74.165016 years.
That is the year: 2043.165039

Table 1

time with %	percent	year
	15	12
	30	23
	45	30
	60	34
	75	38
	90	41

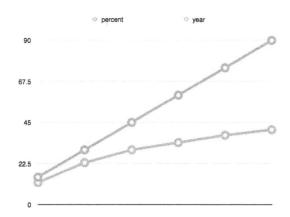

We see as percent progress (blue) climbs steady, the time to do it becomes less and less.

```c
#include <stdio.h>
#include <math.h>
int main (void)
{
printf("\n");
float object, Tzero, T, time, L;
int n;
printf("If we use alphacentauri as the key to our model,\n");
printf("for modeling the future, then our task has been reduced,\n");
printf("through the work I have done, to quite a simple one.\n");
printf("growthrate=k=0.0621, objective=log 100/log e = 4.6
achievements,\n");
printf("Tzero=1969 when we landed on the moon, which at 2009 is
0.552=.0.12(4.6)\n");
printf("1/0.55 = 1.8=9/5 = R/r = Au/Ag, putting us in the age of
gold:silver\n");
printf("Our equation is then, Time=(Object Achieved)/(Achievements/
year)\n");
printf("\n");

do
{
printf("How many simulations would you like to run (10 max)? ");
scanf("%d", &n);
}
while (n>10 && n<=0);
for (int i=1; i<=n; i++)
{
do
{
printf("What is percent develpment towards objective(0-100)? ");
scanf("%f", &object);
}
while (n<0 && n>100);
printf("What is the starting point (year:enter 1969) ?");
scanf("%f", &Tzero);
L= ((log10 (object))/((log10 (2.718)))));
T=L/(0.0621);
time= Tzero+T;
printf("Time to object=%f years.\n", T);
printf("That is the year: %f\n", time);
printf("\n");
}
}
```

The Program In Python

```python
import math
object=float(raw_input("Enter percent development towards objective: "));
Tzero=float(raw_input("Enter the starting point (enter 1969): "));
L=math.log10(object)/math.log10(2.718);
T=L/(0.0621);
Time=Tzero+T;
print("Time to objective is: " + str(T) + "years");
print("That is the year: " + str(Time));
```

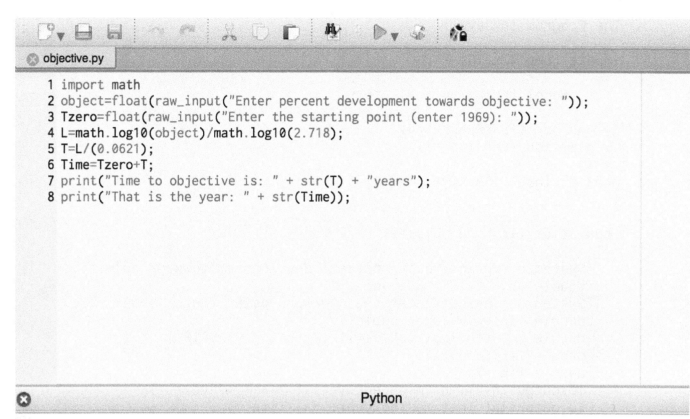

```
  1 import math
  2 object=float(raw_input("Enter percent development towards objective: "));
  3 Tzero=float(raw_input("Enter the starting point (enter 1969): "));
  4 L=math.log10(object)/math.log10(2.718);
  5 T=L/(0.0621);
  6 Time=Tzero+T;
  7 print("Time to objective is: " + str(T) + "years");
  8 print("That is the year: " + str(Time));
```

Python

```
Welcome to Canopy's interactive data-analysis environment!
 with pylab-backend set to: qt
Type '?' for more information.

In [1]: %run "/Users/ianbeardsley/Desktop/objective.py"

Enter percent development towards objective: 100

Enter the starting point (enter 1969): 1969
Time to objective is: 74.1650196331years
That is the year: 2043.16501963

In [2]: %run "/Users/ianbeardsley/Desktop/objective.py"

Enter percent development towards objective: 50

Enter the starting point (enter 1969): 1969
Time to objective is: 63.0020718638years
That is the year: 2032.00207186

In [3]:
```

The Program In Java

```java
import comp102x.IO;
/**
 * We model the human trajectory.
 *
 * @author (Ian Beardsley)
 * @version (version 01)
 */
public class objective
{

  public static void object()
  {
    System.out.print("Enter percent development towards objective: ");
    double object=IO.inputDouble();
    System.out.print("Enter the starting point (enter 1969): ");
    double Tzero=IO.inputDouble();
    double L=(Math.log10(object))/(Math.log10(2.718));
    double T=L/(0.0621);
    double Time=Tzero+T;
    IO.outputln("Time to objective is: " + T + "years");
    IO.outputln("That is the year: " + Time );
}
}
```

```
┌─────────────────────────────────────────────────────────────┐
│  ● ● ●        BlueJ: Terminal Window - COMP 102x Lab 02       │
├─────────────────────────────────────────────────────────────┤
│  Enter percent development towards objective: 25              │
│  Enter the starting point (enter 1969): 1969                 │
│  Time to objective is: 51.83912409451816years                │
│  That is the year: 2020.8391240945182                        │
│  Enter percent development towards objective: 100            │
│  Enter the starting point (enter 1969): 1969                 │
│  Time to objective is: 74.16501963308473years                │
│  That is the year: 2043.1650196330847                        │
│  Enter percent development towards objective: 75             │
│  Enter the starting point (enter 1969): 1969                 │
│  Time to objective is: 69.53197770634105years                │
│  That is the year: 2038.531977706341                         │
│                                                               │
│                                                               │
│                                                               │
│                                                               │
│                                                               │
│                                                               │
└─────────────────────────────────────────────────────────────┘
```

Here we run the program in Java:

If we are to have any method for determining p and q, probabilities
away from and, towards success, we have to consider the chief elements
that whose state need to be assessed. The number one thing to
consider is climate. Thus we present a comprehensive theory of
climate:

Yes ◊

Full Pa

for modeling the future, then our task has been reduced,
through the work I have done, to quite a simple one.
growthrate=k=0.0621, objective=log 100/log e = 4.6
achievements,
Tzero=1969 when we landed on the moon, which at 2009
is 0.552=.0.12(4.6)
1/0.55 = 1.8=9/5 = R/r = Au/Ag, putting us in the age
of gold:silver
Our equation is then, Time=(Object Achieved)/
(Achievements/year)

How many simulations would you like to run (10 max)?
4
What is percent develpment towards objective(0-100)?
40
What is the starting point (year:enter 1969) ?1969
Time to object=59.408405 years.
That is the year: 2028.408447

What is percent develpment towards objective(0-100)?
85
What is the starting point (year:enter 1969) ?1984
Time to object=71.547699 years.
That is the year: 2055.547607

What is percent develpment towards objective(0-100)?
100
What is the starting point (year:enter 1969) ?1990
Time to object=74.165016 years.
That is the year: 2064.165039

What is percent develpment towards objective(0-100)?
90
What is the starting point (year:enter 1969) ?1990
Time to object=72.468216 years.
That is the year: 2062.468262

Project Docu

Project Forn

Organizati

Class Pre

Text Settings

Indent Usi

Widt

Source Cont

Reposito

Ty

Current Bran

Versi

C
To

T
in

P

space odyssey novels

```
Last login: Mon Apr 11 03:58:33 on ttys000
Claires-MBP:~ ianbeardsley$ /Users/ianbeardsley/Desktop/The\ Anomaly/
projectfuture\ copy ; exit;

If we use alphacentauri as the key to our model,
for modeling the future, then our task has been reduced,
through the work I have done, to quite a simple one.
growthrate=k=0.0621, objective=log 100/log e = 4.6 achievements,
Tzero=1969 when we landed on the moon, which at 2009 is 0.552=.
0.12(4.6)
1/0.55 = 1.8=9/5 = R/r = Au/Ag, putting us in the age of gold:silver
Our equation is then, Time=(Object Achieved)/(Achievements/year)

How many simulations would you like to run (10 max)? 5
What is percent develpment towards objective(0-100)? 7.4
What is the starting point (year:enter 1969) ?1969
Time to object=32.233292 years.
That is the year: 2001.233276
```
humans land on moon — novel 1

```
What is percent develpment towards objective(0-100)? 84
What is the starting point (year:enter 1969) ?1990
Time to object=71.357109 years.
That is the year: 2061.357178
```
graduated high school — novel 3

```
What is percent develpment towards objective(0-100)? 100
What is the starting point (year:enter 1969) ?2927
Time to object=74.165016 years.
That is the year: 3001.165039
```
novel 4 (conclusion)

```
What is percent develpment towards objective(0-100)? 50
What is the starting point (year:enter 1969) ?2001
Time to object=63.002071 years.
That is the year: 2064.001953

What is percent develpment towards objective(0-100)? 45
What is the starting point (year:enter 1969) ?2001
Time to object=61.305267 years.
That is the year: 2062.305176

logout

[Process completed]
```

```
Last login: Mon Apr 11 04:05:45 on ttys000
Claires-MBP:~ ianbeardsley$ /Users/ianbeardsley/Desktop/The\ Anomaly/
projectfuture\ copy ; exit;

If we use alphacentauri as the key to our model,
for modeling the future, then our task has been reduced,
through the work I have done, to quite a simple one.
growthrate=k=0.0621, objective=log 100/log e = 4.6 achievements,
Tzero=1969 when we landed on the moon, which at 2009 is 0.552=.
0.12(4.6)
1/0.55 = 1.8=9/5 = R/r = Au/Ag, putting us in the age of gold:silver
Our equation is then, Time=(Object Achieved)/(Achievements/year)

How many simulations would you like to run (10 max)? 3
What is percent develpment towards objective(0-100)? 2
What is the starting point (year:enter 1969) ?2001
Time to object=11.162948 years.
That is the year: 2012.162964
```
mayan calendar
```
What is percent develpment towards objective(0-100)? 1.8
What is the starting point (year:enter 1969) ?2001
Time to object=9.466145 years.
That is the year: 2010.466187
```
novel 2
```
What is percent develpment towards objective(0-100)?
```

Table 1

objective	time	development X 10
	1	74
	10	18
	61	840
	1001	1000

○ time   ○ development X 10

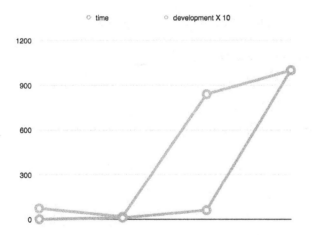

The Robot Series, The Foundation Series, and The Empire Series of Isaac Asimov are really one story. Because it begins with The Robot Series, where some humans have left earth for the nearby stars, The Spacers, as they are called, and because the Earth detective is called upon to solve a mystery on one of these outer worlds, he becomes respected by them, and ultimately through the engineering of a robot, he is maneuvered into leading a second wave of settling the this time the distant stars, Elijah Bailey becomes the one who leads to the human settlement of the Galaxy and, although dates are given at this point in the Foundation Novels by a fictional Galactic Calendar, we know when it started, because the earth calendar we use was used by him. Careful reading of the novels allows when one to figure out a galactic timeline for the history of the galaxy as was computed and is available online. This allows me to use my computer programs I wrote, to model the Asimovian Trajectory. Because Galactic Era and Foundation Era maintain the Earth year duration closely (The people not knowing its origins), we can calculate G.E. and F.E. dates for their Christ Era Equivalents.

We begin where we left off, with the intersection of the Sierra Waters of Paul Levinson (The Plot to Save Socrates) , and the computer called The Brain of Isaac Asimov (I, Robot).

1) (2042-2044) Sierra Waters handed newly discovered Ancient Greek Manuscript (2042). Ian Beardsley predicts hyperdrive for 2043 applying mathematics to the nearest star system. The Brain, in I, Robot, invents hyperdrive in 2044.
2) 3500 C.E. Spacetown, Earth; Elijah Bailey works with robot R. Daneel Olivaw to solve murder mystery, in The Caves of Steel, by Isaac Asimov.
3) (3505) Second wave of immigration from Earth led by Ben Bailey. Tensions arise between Spacer Worlds and Settler Worlds.
4) (12000 C.E) At center of Galaxy Trantor forms Republic of five worlds and the origins of humans are forgotten (The Currents of Space).
5) 12,500 C.E. is 1 G.E.
6) (12,067 Galactic Era or G.E. and Foundation Era or 1 F.E.) Puts 1 F.E. at about 12500+12067=24,567 C.E. = 1 F.E. or Foundation Era. Galactic Empire then lasted about 24,567-12.500=12,67 years.
7) (12500 C.E. or 1 G.E.: Galactic Era) Trantor becomes the seat of the Galactic Empire. (Read The Currents of Space).
8) (3 F.E.:Foundation Era) Hari Seldon who created the foundation on Terminus, dies.
9) (300 F.E.) The Mule, a mutant with mental powers overthrows the Foundation. This is 300 FE + 24,567 CE = 24,867 years after Christ Era (CE).
10) (310 F.E.) The Mule is defeated and The Foundation is restored democratic rule over the galaxy.
11) (498 F.E.) Golan Trevize choses the Gaia Model for the Galaxy, over The Foundation.) 498 +24,567 = 25,065 CE.

We have:

Sierra Waters and the Brain: 2043
Earth visits spacers (Elijah Bailey): 3500
Second Wave of Emigration (The Settlers): 3505
Trantor forms republic: 12,000
Trantor become seat of the galaxy: 12,500
Foundation Era: 24,570
The Mule: 24,867
Gaia is established: 25,065

The online timeline is much more detailed, but, from having read all the novels, I was able to choose out of it the major events a transitions leading to the ideal galactic society, called Gaia. Let us now make a graph that shows the rate at which humanity progresses towards this Gaia:

Table 1

event	CE						
sierra waters	2043						
spacers	3500						
settlers	3505						
trantor	12500						
foundation	24570						
the mule	24867						
gaia	25065						

 CE

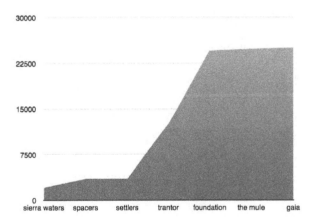

R = Solar Radius
r= lunar orbital radius
Au = gold
Ag = silver

R/r = Au/Ag = 9/5

(9/5)(4) = 7.2
Mars = 4
The earth precesses through one degree in 72 years
0.72 = Venus orbital radius in Astronomical Units (AU)

harmonic mean: Ga; As = 72.23
geometric mean: Ga; As = 72.27
23=Manuel Number
27=Manuel Number

23X27=621=L=Levinson's Number

Ga=69.72
As=74.92
Ga=Gallium
As=Arsenic

Ga and As are doping agents for making diodes, transistors, integrated circuitry,...the operational components of AI.

a) 2(69.72)(74.92)=10446.8448
b) (69.72)+(74.92)=144.64
c) a/b=72.2265~72.23
d) (69.72)(74.92)=5223.4224
e) sqrt(5223.4224)=72.27324816

9/5 connects pi to phi: 3.141+1.618=4.759
7=(9+5)/2

360/5=72 360-72=288
288/360 = 8/10 (8/10)+1 = 9/5

360/6 = 60 360-60-60=240
240/360 = 2/3 (2/3)+1 = 5/3

360/6=60 360-60 = 300
300/360 = 5/6 (5/6)+1 = 11/6

9/5, 5/3, 11/6

9/5: 5, 14, 23, 32,...
    1.8, 3.6, 5.4, 7.2,...

5/3: 8, 13, 18, 23,...
    1.7, 3.3, 5, 6.7

11/6: 6, 17, 28, 39
    11/6, 11/3, 11/2, 22/3

9/5: $a_n = 7.2n - 4$
5/3: $a_n = 3.3n + 3$
11/6: $a_n = 9n - 5$

=> <5/36, -10/33, -1/9> (Here we have inverted the coefficients of the equation of the plane)

sqrt(((5/36)^2) + ((20/33)^2)) = 0.0621 = Levinson's number~phi=0.618~0.62

Here we have eliminated n and taken the gradient to find the normal to the plane. The figure in the square root is the right ascension vector pointing to the constellation Aquila.

sin 45 = (sqrt(2))/2
(sqrt(2))/2= M = manuel's number

621=L= levinson's number

ML=440
440=standard concert pitch

23, 27 = Manuel Numbers
23X27=621=L

0.0621, Levinson's number is a growth rate for progress, There are 0.621 miles in a kilometer (km) and 1 km=1/10,000 of the distance from the pole to the equator. 0.0621 is the novelty rating in the McKenna Timewave for the year humans first set foot on the moon.

Genesis Source Code

Ian Beardsley

bioplanet (code)

Ian Beardsley

© 2016

```c
#include<stdio.h>
#include<math.h>
int main(void)
{
printf("\n");
printf("\n");
printf("Here we use a single atomospheric layer with no\n");
printf("convection for the planet to be in an equilibrium\n");
printf("state.  That is to say, the temperature stays\n");
printf("steady by heat gain and loss with radiative\n");
printf("heat transfer alone.\n");
printf("The habitable zone is calculated using the idea\n");
printf("that the earth is in the habitable zone for a\n");
printf("star like the Sun. That is, if a star is 100\n");
printf("times brighter than the Sun, then the habitable\n");
printf("zone for that star is ten times further from\n");
printf("it than the Earth is from the Sun because ten\n");
printf("squared is 100\n");
printf("\n");

float s, a, l, b, r, AU, N, root, number, answer, C, F;
printf("We determine the surface temperature of a planet.\n");
printf("What is the luminosity of the star in solar luminosities? ");
scanf("%f", &s);
printf("What is the albedo of the planet (0-1)?" );
scanf("%f", &a);
printf("What is the distance from the star in AU? ");
scanf("%f", &AU);
r=1.5E11*AU;
l=3.9E26*s;
b=l/(4*3.141*r*r);

N=(1-a)*b/(4*(5.67E-8));
root=sqrt(N);
number=sqrt(root);
answer=1.189*(number);
printf("\n");
printf("\n");
printf("The surface temperature of the planet is: %f K\n", answer);
C=answer-273;
F=(C*1.8)+32;
printf("That is %f C, or %f F", C, F);
printf("\n");
float joules;
joules=(3.9E26*s);
printf("The luminosity of the star in joules per second is: %.
2fE25\n", joules/1E25);
float HZ;
HZ=sqrt(joules/3.9E26);
```

```c
printf("The habitable zone of the star in AU is: %f\n", HZ);
printf("Flux at planet is %.2f times that at earth.\n", b/1370);
printf("That is %.2f Watts per square meter\n", b);




printf("\n");
printf("\n");

printf("In this simulation we use a two layer atmospheric model\n");
printf("where equilibrium is maintained by both radiative heat\n");
printf("transfer and convection,\n");
printf("\n");

printf("This program finds the temperature of a planet\n");
float L0,sun,S0,r0,R,S,A,sigma,TE,delta,sTe4,sTs4;
float result, answer2, c, f, x;
printf("Luminosity of the star in solar luminosities? ");
scanf("%f", &L0);
printf("Planet distance from the star in AU? ");
scanf("%f", &r0);
printf("What is the albedo of the planet (0-1)? ");
scanf("%f", &A);
printf("What is the temp dif between layers in kelvin? ");
scanf("%f", &delta);
sun=3.9E26;
S0=L0*sun;
R=(1.5E11)*r0;
S=(S0)/((4)*(3.141)*R*R);
sigma=5.67E-8;
TE=(sqrt(sqrt((((1-A)*S*(0.25))/sigma))));
x=delta/TE;
sTe4=(1-A)*S/4;
sTs4=3*(sTe4)-(sTe4)*(2-(1+x)*(1+x)*(1+x)*(1+x))-
(sTe4)*(1+(1+x)*(1+x)*(1+x)*(1+x)-(1+2*x)*(1+2*x)*(1+2*x)*(1+2*x));
result=(sTs4)/(sigma);
answer2=sqrt((sqrt(result)));
printf("\n");
printf("\n");
printf("planet surface temp is: %f K\n", answer2);
c=answer2-273;
f=(1.8)*c+32;
printf("That is %f C, or %f F\n", c, f);
printf("flux at planet is %f watts per square meter\n", S);
printf("\n");
printf("\n");
}
```

modelplanet (code)

Ian Beardsley

© 2016

```c
#include <stdio.h>
#include <math.h>
int main(void)
{
printf("\n");
printf("We input the radii of the layers of a planet,...\n");
printf("and their corresponding densities,...\n");
printf("to determine the planet's composition.\n");
printf("Iron Core Density Fe=7.87 g/cm^3\n");
printf("Lithosphere Density Ni = 8.91 g/cm^3\n");
printf("Mantle Density Si=2.33 g/cm^3\n");
printf("Earth Radius = 6,371 km\n");
printf("Earth Mass = 5.972E24 Kg\n");
printf("\n");
float r1=0.00, r2=0.00, r3=0.00, p1=0.00, p2=0.00, p3=0.00;
printf("what is r1, the radius of the core in km? ");
scanf("%f", &r1);
printf("what is p1, its density in g/cm^3? ");
scanf("%f", &p1);
printf("what is r2, outer edge of layer two in km? ");
scanf("%f", &r2);
printf("what is p2, density of layer two in g/cm^3? ");
scanf("%f", &p2);
printf("what is r3, the radius of layer 3 in km? ");
scanf("%f", &r3);
printf("what is p3, density of layer three in g/cm^3? ");
scanf("%f", &p3);
printf("\n");
printf("\n");
printf("r1=%.2f, r2=%.2f, r3=%.2f, p1=%.2f, p2=%.2f, p3=%.2f \n",
r1,r2,r3,p1,p2,p3);
printf("\n");

float R1, v1, m1, M1;
{
R1=(r1)*(1000.00)*(100.00);
v1=(3.141)*(R1)*(R1)*(R1)*(4.00)/(3.00);
m1=(p1)*(v1);
M1=m1/1000.00;
printf("the core has a mass of %.2f E23 Kg\n", M1/1E23);
printf("thickness of core is %.2f \n", r1);
}
float R2, v2, m2, M2;
{
R2=(r2)*(1000.00)*(100.00);
v2=(3.141)*(R2*R2*R2-R1*R1*R1)*(4.00)/(3.00);
m2=(p2)*(v2);
M2=m2/1000.00;
printf("layer two has a mass of %.2f E23 Kg\n", M2/1E23);
```

```
printf("layer two thickness is %.2f \n", r2-r1);
}
float R3, v3, m3, M3;
{
R3=(r3)*(1000.00)*(100.00);
v3=(3.141)*(R3*R3*R3-R2*R2*R2)*(4.00)/(3.00);
m3=(p3)*(v3);
M3=m3/1000.00;
printf("layer three has a mass of %.2f E23 Kg\n", M3/1E23);
printf("layer three thickness is %.2f \n", r3-r2);
}
printf("\n");
printf("\n");
printf("the mass of the planet is %.2f E24 Kg\n", (M1+M2+M3)/1E24);
}
```

modelocean (code)

Ian Beardsley

© 2016

```c
#include <stdio.h>
int main (void)
{
int option;
printf("\n");
printf("The surface area of the earth is 510E6 square km.\n");
printf("About three quarters of that is ocean.\n");
printf("Half the surface area of the earth is receiving sunlight at
any given moment.\n");
printf("0.75*510E6/2 = 200E6 square km recieving light from the sun.
\n");
printf("There is about one gram of water per cubic cm.\n");
printf("\n");
printf("Is the section of water you are considering on the order of:
\n");
printf("1 a waterhole\n");
printf("2 a pond \n");
printf("3 the ocean\n");
scanf("%d", &option);

{
float area, depth, cubic, density=0.000, mass=0.000;
printf("How many square meters of water are warmed? ");
scanf("%f", &area);
printf("How many meters deep is the water warmed? ");
scanf("%f", &depth);
cubic=area*depth;
density=100*100*100; //grams per cubic meter//
mass=(density)*(cubic);
if (option==2)
{
printf("That is %.3f E3 cubic meters of water. \n", cubic/1E3);
printf("%.3f cubic meters of water has a mass of about %.3f E6 grams.
\n", cubic, mass/1E6);
printf("\n");
printf("\n");
}
if (option==1)
{
printf("That is %.3f cubic meters of water.\n", cubic);
printf("%.3f cubic meters of water has a mass of about %.3f E3 grams.
\n", cubic, mass/1E3);
}
if (option==3)
{
printf("That is %.3f E3 cubic meters of water.\n", cubic/1E3);
printf("%.3f E3 m^3 of water has a mass of about %.3f E12 g\n", cubic/
1E3, mass/1E12);
printf("\n");
```

```
}
}
printf("\n");
float reduction, incident, energy, watts, square, deep, volume, vol,
densiti, matter;
float temp, increase, temperature;
printf("The specific heat of water is one gram per calorie-degree
centigrade.\n");
printf("One calorie is 4.8400 Joules.\n");
printf("The light entering the earth is 1,370 Joules per second per
square meter.\n");
printf("That is 1,370 watts per square meter.\n");
printf("By what percent is the light entering reduced by clouds? (0-1)
");
scanf("%f", &reduction);
incident=reduction*1370;
printf("Incident radiation is: %.3f watts per square meter.\n",
incident);
printf("\n");
printf("The body of water is exposed to the sunlight from 10:00 AM to
2:00 PM.\n");
printf("That is four hours which are 14,400 seconds.\n");
watts=14400*incident;
printf("How many square meters of water are to be considered? ");
scanf("%f", &square);
printf("How deep is the water heated (in meters)? ");
scanf("%f", &deep);
volume=deep*square; //volume in cubic meters//
vol=volume*100*100*100; //volume in cubic centimeters//
printf("The volume of water in cubic meters is: %.3f\n", volume);
printf("That is %.3f E3 cubic centimeters.\n", vol/1E3);
densiti=1.00; //density in grams per cubic cm//
matter=densiti*vol; //grams of water//
printf("That is %.3f E3 grams of water in %.3f cubic meters of water.
\n", matter/1E3, volume);
energy=watts*square/4.84;
printf("That is %.3f cubic meters heated by %.3f calories\n", volume,
energy);
printf("What is the intitial temperature of the body of water? ");
scanf("%f", &temp);
increase=energy/(matter*temp);
temperature=increase+temp;
printf("The temperature of the body of water has increased; %.3f
degrees C.\n", increase);
printf("That means the temperature of the body of water is: %.3f
degrees C.\n", temperature);
}
```

starsystem (code)

Ian Beardsley

© 2016

```c
#include<stdio.h>
#include<math.h>
int main(void)
{
printf("\n");
printf("\n");
printf("Here we use a single atomospheric layer with no\n");
printf("convection for the planet to be in an equilibrium\n");
printf("state.  That is to say, the temperature stays\n");
printf("steady by heat gain and loss with radiative\n");
printf("heat transfer alone.\n");
printf("The habitable zone is calculated using the idea\n");
printf("that the earth is in the habitable zone for a\n");
printf("star like the Sun. That is, if a star is 100\n");
printf("times brighter than the Sun, then the habitable\n");
printf("zone for that star is ten times further from\n");
printf("it than the Earth is from the Sun because ten\n");
printf("squared is 100\n");
printf("\n");

float s, a, l, b, r, AU, N, root, number, answer, C, F;
printf("We determine the surface temperature of a planet.\n");
printf("What is the luminosity of the star in solar luminosities? ");
scanf("%f", &s);
printf("What is the albedo of the planet (0-1)?" );
scanf("%f", &a);
printf("What is the distance from the star in AU? ");
scanf("%f", &AU);
r=1.5E11*AU;
l=3.9E26*s;
b=l/(4*3.141*r*r);

N=(1-a)*b/(4*(5.67E-8));
root=sqrt(N);
number=sqrt(root);
answer=1.189*(number);
printf("\n");
printf("\n");
printf("The surface temperature of the planet is: %f K\n", answer);
C=answer-273;
F=(C*1.8)+32;
printf("That is %f C, or %f F", C, F);
printf("\n");
float joules;
joules=(3.9E26*s);
printf("The luminosity of the star in joules per second is: %.
2fE25\n", joules/1E25);
float HZ;
HZ=sqrt(joules/3.9E26);
```

```
printf("The habitable zone of the star in AU is: %f\n", HZ);
printf("Flux at planet is %.2f times that at earth.\n", b/1370);
printf("That is %.2f Watts per square meter\n", b);



printf("\n");
printf("\n");

printf("In this simulation we use a two layer atmospheric model\n");
printf("where equilibrium is maintained by both radiative heat\n");
printf("transfer and convection,\n");
printf("\n");

printf("This program finds the temperature of a planet\n");
float L0,sun,S0,r0,R,S,A,sigma,TE,delta,sTe4,sTs4;
float result, answer2, c, f, x;
printf("Luminosity of the star in solar luminosities? ");
scanf("%f", &L0);
printf("Planet distance from the star in AU? ");
scanf("%f", &r0);
printf("What is the albedo of the planet (0-1)? ");
scanf("%f", &A);
printf("What is the temp dif between layers in kelvin? ");
scanf("%f", &delta);
sun=3.9E26;
S0=L0*sun;
R=(1.5E11)*r0;
S=(S0)/((4)*(3.141)*R*R);
sigma=5.67E-8;
TE=(sqrt(sqrt((((1-A)*S*(0.25))/sigma))));
x=delta/TE;
sTe4=(1-A)*S/4;
sTs4=3*(sTe4)-(sTe4)*(2-(1+x)*(1+x)*(1+x)*(1+x))-
(sTe4)*(1+(1+x)*(1+x)*(1+x)*(1+x)-(1+2*x)*(1+2*x)*(1+2*x)*(1+2*x));
result=(sTs4)/(sigma);
answer2=sqrt((sqrt(result)));
printf("\n");
printf("\n");
printf("planet surface temp is: %f K\n", answer2);
c=answer2-273;
f=(1.8)*c+32;
printf("That is %f C, or %f F\n", c, f);
printf("flux at planet is %f watts per square meter\n", S);
printf("\n");
printf("\n");
```

```c
    printf("\n");
    printf("We input the radii of the layers of a planet,...\n");
    printf("and their corresponding densities,...\n");
    printf("to determine the planet's composition.\n");
    printf("Iron Core Density Fe=7.87 g/cm^3\n");
    printf("Lithosphere Density Ni = 8.91 g/cm^3\n");
    printf("Mantle Density Si=2.33 g/cm^3\n");
    printf("Earth Radius = 6,371 km\n");
    printf("Earth Mass = 5.972E24 Kg\n");
    printf("\n");
    float r1=0.00, r2=0.00, r3=0.00, p1=0.00, p2=0.00, p3=0.00;
    printf("what is r1, the radius of the core in km? ");
    scanf("%f", &r1);
    printf("what is p1, its density in g/cm^3? ");
    scanf("%f", &p1);
    printf("what is r2, outer edge of layer two in km? ");
    scanf("%f", &r2);
    printf("what is p2, density of layer two in g/cm^3? ");
    scanf("%f", &p2);
    printf("what is r3, the radius of layer 3 in km? ");
    scanf("%f", &r3);
    printf("what is p3, density of layer three in g/cm^3? ");
    scanf("%f", &p3);
    printf("\n");
    printf("\n");
    printf("r1=%.2f, r2=%.2f, r3=%.2f, p1=%.2f, p2=%.2f, p3=%.2f \n",
r1,r2,r3,p1,p2,p3);
    printf("\n");

    float R1, v1, m1, M1;
    {
        R1=(r1)*(1000.00)*(100.00);
        v1=(3.141)*(R1)*(R1)*(R1)*(4.00)/(3.00);
        m1=(p1)*(v1);
        M1=m1/1000.00;
        printf("the core has a mass of %.2f E23 Kg\n", M1/1E23);
        printf("thickness of core is %.2f \n", r1);
    }
    float R2, v2, m2, M2;
    {
        R2=(r2)*(1000.00)*(100.00);
        v2=(3.141)*(R2*R2*R2-R1*R1*R1)*(4.00)/(3.00);
        m2=(p2)*(v2);
        M2=m2/1000.00;
        printf("layer two has a mass of %.2f E23 Kg\n", M2/1E23);
        printf("layer two thickness is %.2f \n", r2-r1);
    }
    float R3, v3, m3, M3;
    {
```

```
        R3=(r3)*(1000.00)*(100.00);
        v3=(3.141)*(R3*R3*R3-R2*R2*R2)*(4.00)/(3.00);
        m3=(p3)*(v3);
        M3=m3/1000.00;
        printf("layer three has a mass of %.2f E23 Kg\n", M3/1E23);
        printf("layer three thickness is %.2f \n", r3-r2);
    }
    printf("\n");
    printf("\n");
    printf("the mass of the planet is %.2f E24 Kg\n", (M1+M2+M3)/
1E24);


    int option;
    printf("\n");
    printf("The surface area of the earth is 510E6 square km.\n");
    printf("About three quarters of that is ocean.\n");
    printf("Half the surface area of the earth is receiving sunlight
at any given moment.\n");
    printf("0.75*510E6/2 = 200E6 square km recieving light from the
sun.\n");
    printf("There is about one gram of water per cubic cm.\n");
    printf("\n");
    printf("Is the section of water you are considering on the order
of: \n");
    printf("1 a waterhole\n");
    printf("2 a pond \n");
    printf("3 the ocean\n");
    scanf("%d", &option);

    {
        float area, depth, cubic, density=0.000, mass=0.000;
        printf("How many square meters of water are warmed? ");
        scanf("%f", &area);
        printf("How many meters deep is the water warmed? ");
        scanf("%f", &depth);
        cubic=area*depth;
        density=100*100*100; //grams per cubic meter//
        mass=(density)*(cubic);
        if (option==2)
        {
            printf("That is %.3f E3 cubic meters of water. \n", cubic/
1E3);
            printf("%.3f cubic meters of water has a mass of about %.
3f E6 grams.\n", cubic, mass/1E6);
            printf("\n");
            printf("\n");
        }
        if (option==1)
```

```
        {
                printf("That is %.3f cubic meters of water.\n", cubic);
                printf("%.3f cubic meters of water has a mass of about %.
3f E3 grams.\n", cubic, mass/1E3);
        }
        if (option==3)
        {
                printf("That is %.3f E3 cubic meters of water.\n", cubic/
1E3);
                printf("%.3f E3 m^3 of water has a mass of about %.3f E12
g\n", cubic/1E3, mass/1E12);
                printf("\n");
        }
    }
    printf("\n");
    float reduction, incident, energy, watts, square, deep, volume,
vol, densiti, matter;
    float temp, increase, temperature;
    printf("The specific heat of water is one gram per calorie-degree
centigrade.\n");
    printf("One calorie is 4.8400 Joules.\n");
    printf("The light entering the earth is 1,370 Joules per second
per square meter.\n");
    printf("That is 1,370 watts per square meter.\n");
    printf("By what percent is the light entering reduced by clouds?
(0-1) ");
    scanf("%f", &reduction);
    incident=reduction*1370;
    printf("Incident radiation is: %.3f watts per square meter.\n",
incident);
    printf("\n");
    printf("The body of water is exposed to the sunlight from 10:00 AM
to 2:00 PM.\n");
    printf("That is four hours which are 14,400 seconds.\n");
    watts=14400*incident;
    printf("How many square meters of water are to be considered? ");
    scanf("%f", &square);
    printf("How deep is the water heated (in meters)? ");
    scanf("%f", &deep);
    volume=deep*square; //volume in cubic meters//
    vol=volume*100*100*100; //volume in cubic centimeters//
    printf("The volume of water in cubic meters is: %.3f\n", volume);
    printf("That is %.3f E3 cubic centimeters.\n", vol/1E3);
    densiti=1.00; //density in grams per cubic cm//
    matter=densiti*vol; //grams of water//
    printf("That is %.3f E3 grams of water in %.3f cubic meters of
water.\n", matter/1E3, volume);
    energy=watts*square/4.84;
```

```
    printf("That is %.3f cubic meters heated by %.3f calories\n",
volume, energy);
    printf("What is the intitial temperature of the body of water? ");
    scanf("%f", &temp);
    increase=energy/(matter*temp);
    temperature=increase+temp;
    printf("The temperature of the body of water has increased; %.3f
degrees C.\n", increase);
    printf("That means the temperature of the body of water is: %.3f
degrees C.\n", temperature);
}
```

modelfuture (code)

Ian Beardsley

© 2016

```c
#include <stdio.h>
#include <math.h>
int main (void)
{
printf("\n");
int N, r;
double u, v, y, z;
double t,loga, ratio;
int n1, n2;
char name[15];
float W,fact=1,fact2=1,fact3=1,a,g,rate,T,T1;
double x,W2;
printf("(p^n1)(q^n2)[W=N!/(n1!)(n2!)]");
printf("\n");
printf("x=e^(c*t)");
printf("\n");
printf("W is the probability of landing on the star in N jumps.\n");
printf("N=n1+n2, n1=number of one light year jumps left,\n");
printf("n2=number of one light year jumps right.\n");
printf("What is 1, the nearest whole number of light years to the
star, and\n");
printf("2, what is the star's name?\n");
printf("Enter 1: ");
scanf("%i", &r);
printf("Enter 2: ");
scanf("%s", name);
printf("Star name: %s\n", name);
printf("Distance: %i\n", r);
printf("What is n1? ");
scanf("%i", &n1);
printf("What is n2? ");
scanf("%i", &n2);
printf("Since N=n1+n2, N=%i\n", n1+n2);
N=n1+n2;
printf("What is the probability, p(u), of jumping to the left? ");
scanf("%lf", &u);
printf("What is the probability, p(v), of jumpint to the left? ");
scanf("%lf", &v);
printf("What is the probability, q(y), of jumping to the right? ");
scanf("%lf", &y);
printf("What is the probability, q(z), of jumping to the right? ");
scanf("%lf", &z);
printf("p=u:v");
printf("\n");
printf("q=y:z");
printf("\n");
for (int i=1; i<=N; i++)
{
fact = fact*i;
```

```c
printf("N factorial = %f\n", fact);

a=pow(u/v,n1)*pow(y/z,n2);
}
for (int j=1; j<=n1; j++)
{
fact2 = fact2*j;
printf("n1 factorial = %f\n", fact2);
}
for (int k=1; k<=n2; k++)
{
fact3 = fact3*k;
printf("n2 factorial = %f\n", fact3);

x=2.718*2.718*2.718*2.718*2.718;
g=sqrt(x);
W=a*fact/(fact2*fact3);
printf("W=%f percent\n", W*100);
W2=100*W;
printf("W=%.2f percent rounded to nearest integral\n", round(W2));
}
{
printf("What is t in years, the time over which the growth occurs? ");
scanf("%lf", &t);
loga=log10(round(W*100));
printf("log(W)=%lf\n", loga);
ratio=loga/t;
printf("loga/t=%lf\n", ratio);
rate=ratio/0.4342; //0.4342 = log e//
printf("growthrate constant=%lf\n", rate);
printf("log 100 = 2, log e = 0.4342, therfore\n");
printf("T=2/[(0.4342)(growthrate)]\n");
T=2/((0.4342)*(rate));
printf("T=%.2f years\n", T);
printf("What was the begin year for the period of growth? ");
scanf("%f", &T1);
printf("Object achieved in %.2f\n", T+T1);
}
}
```

stellar (python)

Ian Beardsley

© 2016

```python
print("We determine the surface temperature of a planet.")
s=float(raw_input("Enter stellar luminosity in solar luminosities: "))
a=float(raw_input("What is planet albedo (0-1)?: "))
au=float(raw_input("What is the distance from star in AU?: "))
r=(1.5)*(10**11)*au
l=(3.9)*(10**26)*s
b=l/((4.0)*(3.141)*(r**2))
N=((1-a)*b)/(4.0*((5.67)*(10**(-8))))
root=N**(1.0/2.0)
number=root**(1.0/2.0)
answer=1.189*number
print("The surface temperature of the planet is: "+str(answer)+"K")
C=answer-273
F=(9.0/5.0)*C + 32
print("That is " +str(C)+"C")
print("Which is " +str(F)+"F")
joules=3.9*(10**26)*s/1E25
lum=(3.9E26)*s
print("luminosity of star in joules per sec: "+str(joules)+"E25")
HZ=((lum/(3.9*10**26)))**(1.0/2.0)
print("The habitable zone is: "+str(HZ))
flux=b/1370.0
print("Flux at planet is "+str(flux)+" times that at earth")
print("That is " +str(b)+ " watts per square meter")
```

double (python)

Ian Beardsley

, © 2016

```
print("This program finds the temperature of a planet.")
L0=float(raw_input("Luminosity of the star in solar luminosities? "))
sun=3.9E26
S0=L0*sun
r0=float(raw_input("planet distance from star in AU? "))
r=(1.5E11)*r0
S=S0/((4)*(3.141)*(r**2))
a=float(raw_input("What is the albedo of the planet (1-0)?: "))
sigma=5.67E-8
TE=((1-a)*S*(0.25)/(sigma))**(1.0/4.0)
delta=float(raw_input("temp dif between two layers in Kelvin: "))
x=delta/TE
sTe4=(1-a)*S/4
sTs4=3*(sTe4)-(sTe4)*(2-(1+x)**4)-(sTe4)*(1+((1+x)**4)-(1+2*x)**4)
result=(sTs4)/(sigma)
answer=(result)**(1.0/4.0)
print("planet surface temp is: "+ str(answer)+" K")
C=answer-273
F=(1.8)*C+32
print("That is "+str(C)+" C, or "+str(F)+" F")
print("flux at planet is "+ str(S)+" watts per square meter")
```

modelplanet (java)

Ian Beardsley

```java
import comp102x.IO;
/**
 * Here we write a program in java that models the temperature of a
planet for a star
 * of given luminosity.
 * @author (Ian Beardsley)
 * @version (Version 01 March 2016)
 */
public class bioplanet
{


    public static void bioplanet()
    {
        System.out.print("Enter the luminosity of the star in solar
luminosities: ");
        double lum = IO.inputDouble();
        System.out.print("Enter the distance of the planet from the
star in AU: ");
        double r=IO.inputDouble();
        System.out.print("Enter albedo of the planet (0-1): ");
        double a=IO.inputDouble();
        double R=(1.5E11)*r;
        double S=(3.9E26)*lum;
        double b=S/(4*3.141*R*R);
        double N = (1-a)*b/(4*(5.67E-8));
        double root = Math.sqrt(N);
        double number = Math.sqrt(root);
        double answer = 1.189*number;
        IO.outputln("The surface temperature of the planet is:
"+answer+ " K");
        double C = answer - 273;
        double F = 1.8*C + 32;
        IO.outputln("That is: " +C+ " degrees centigrade");
        IO.outputln("Which is: " + F + " degrees Fahrenheit");


    }
}
```

object (code)

Ian Beardsley

© 2016

```c
#include <stdio.h>
int main (void)
{
printf("\n");
float object, Tzero, T, time;
int n;
printf("If we use alphacentauri as the key to our model,\n");
printf("for modeling the future, then our task has been reduced,\n");
printf("through the work I have done, to quite a simple one.\n");
printf("growthrate=k=0.0621, objective=log 100/log e = 4.6
achievements,\n");
printf("Tzero=1969 when we landed on the moon, which at 2009 is
0.552=.0.12(4.6)\n");
printf("1/0.55 = 1.8=9/5 = R/r = Au/Ag, putting us in the age of
gold:silver\n");
printf("Our equation is then, Time=(Object Achieved)/(Achievements/
year)\n");
printf("\n");

do
{
printf("How many simulations would you like to run (10 max)? ");
scanf("%d", &n);
}
while (n>10 && n<=0);
for (int i=1; i<=n; i++)
{
do
{
printf("What is distance to object(0-4.6?) ");
scanf("%f", &object);
}
while (n<=0 && n>=4.6);
printf("What is the starting point (year) ?");
scanf("%f", &Tzero);
T= object/(0.0621);
time= Tzero+T;
printf("Time to object=%f years.\n", T);
printf("That is the year: %f\n", time);
printf("\n");
}
}
```

input (code)

Ian Beardsley

© 2016

```
#include <stdio.h>
#include <math.h>
int main (void)
{
printf("\n");
char s[15], w[15], t[5], b[10];
printf("Sierra Waters\n");
printf("The Brain\n");
printf("Enter Last Name: ");
scanf("%s", w);
printf("Enter First Name: ");
scanf("%s", s);
printf("Enter Name: ");
scanf("%s", b);
printf("Enter Definite Article: ");
scanf("%s", t);
printf("%s, %s: She was handed the newly discovered document in
2042.\n", w, s);
printf("%s, %s: He designed hyperdrive in 2044.\n", b, t);
printf("Between 2042 and 2044 is 2043.\n");
printf("\n");
printf("\n");
float object, Tzero, T, time, L;
int n;
printf("If we use alphacentauri as the key to our model,\n");
printf("for modeling the future, then our task has been reduced,\n");
printf("through the work I have done, to quite a simple one.\n");
printf("growthrate=k=0.0621, objective=log 100/log e = 4.6
achievements,\n");
printf("Tzero=1969 when we landed on the moon, which at 2009 is
0.552=.0.12(4.6)\n");
printf("1/0.55 = 1.8=9/5 = R/r = Au/Ag, putting us in the age of
gold:silver\n");
printf("Our equation is then, Time=(Object Achieved)/(Achievements/
year)\n");
printf("\n");

do
{
printf("How many simulations would you like to run (10 max)? ");
scanf("%d", &n);
}
while (n>10 && n<=0);
for (int i=1; i<=n; i++)
{
do
{
printf("What is percent development towards objective(0-100)? ");
scanf("%f", &object);
```

```c
}
while (n<0 && n>100);
printf("What is the starting point (year:enter 1969) ?");
scanf("%f", &Tzero);
L= ((log10 (object))/((log10 (2.718))));
T=L/(0.0621);
time= Tzero+T;
printf("Time to object=%f years.\n", T);
printf("That is the year: %f\n", time);
}
printf("\n");
printf("If you chose tzero as moon landing (1969), then you found\n");
printf("obect acheived 2043 between Sierra Waters and The Brain.\n");
printf("That time being reached in 74 years after time zero.\n");
printf("If you ran a second simulation again with t zero at 1969, and
\n");
printf("ran the program for the 74 years to hyperdrive reduced by\n");
printf("a factor of ten (that is input 7.4 percent development.)\n");
printf("Then, you found object achieved in 2001, the year of Kubrick's
\n");
printf("Starchild\n");
printf("\n");
}
```

objective (python)

Ian Beardsley

© 2016

```
import math
object=float(raw_input("Enter percent development towards objective:
"));
Tzero=float(raw_input("Enter the starting point (enter 1969): "));
L=math.log10(object)/math.log10(2.718);
T=L/(0.0621);
Time=Tzero+T;
print("Time to objective is: " + str(T) + "years");
print("That is the year: " + str(Time));
```

Ian Beardsley

Running ModelFuture

Star System: Alpha Centauri
Spectral Class: Same As The Sun
Proximity: Nearest Star System
Value For Projecting Human Trajectory: Ideal

The probability of landing at four light years from earth at Alpha Centauri in 10 random leaps of one light year each (to left or right) is given by the equation of a random walk:

{ W }_{ n }({ n }_{ 1 })=\frac { N! }{ { n }_{ 1 }!{ n }_{ 2 }! } { p }^{ n1 }{ q }^{ n2 }\\
N={ n }_{ 1 }+{ n }_{ 2 }\\ q+p=1

$$W_n(n_1) = \frac{N!}{n_1! n_2!} p^{n1} q^{n2}$$

$$N = n_1 + n_2$$

$$q + p = 1$$

To land at plus four we must jump 3 to the left, 7 to the right (n1=3, n2 = 7: 7+3=10):

Using our equation:

$$\frac{(10!)}{(7!)(3!)}(\frac{1}{2})^7(\frac{1}{2})^3 = \frac{3628800}{(5040)(6)}\frac{1}{128}\frac{1}{8} = \frac{120}{1024} = \frac{15}{128} = 0.1171875 \approx 12\%$$

We would be, by this reasoning 12% along in the development towards hyperdrive.

Having calculated that we are 12% along in developing the hyperdrive, we can use the equation for natural growth to estimate when we will have hyperdrive. It is of the form:

$$x(t) = x_0 e^{kt}$$

t is time and k is a growth rate constant which we must determine to solve the equation. In 1969 Neil Armstrong became the first man to walk on the moon. In 2009 the European Space Agency launched the Herschel and Planck telescopes that will see back to near the beginning of the universe. 2009-1969 is 40 years. This allows us to write:

$$12\% = e^{k(40)}$$

$$\log 12 = 40k \log 2.718$$

$$0.026979531 = 0.4342 k$$

$$k = 0.0621$$

We now can write:

$$x(t) = e^{(0.0621)t}$$

$$100\% = e^{(0.0621)t}$$

$$\log 100 = (0.0621) t \log e$$

$$t = 74 \text{ years}$$

$$1969 + 74 \text{ years} = 2043$$

Our reasoning would indicate that we will have hyperdrive in the year 2043.

Study summary:

1. We have a 70% chance of developing hyperdrive without destroying ourselves first.
2. We are 12% along the way in development of hyperdrive.
3. We will have hyperdrive in the year 2043, plus or minus.

Sierra Waters was handed the newly discovered document in 2042.

```
modelfuture
```

When you write a program that gets the same results as you did by
hand, you know you have not made an error. This program, designed to
project the future, is more sophisticated than the work I did by hand
in the Levinson story, because we can now adjust the probabilities, p
and q, and use any destination star we wish. Here is the program,
which I call "model future" (modelfuture.c). I have already written
programs, bioplanet, model planet and model ocean. Have combined them
in one work called star system. They will be presented at the end of
this paper.

For now, here is the code in C for model future, and a sample run that
shows the calculations in the Levinson story, are accurate.

Last login: Tue Apr 5 20:29:12 on ttys000
/Users/ianbeardsley/Desktop/object\ run ; exit;
Claires-MBP:~ ianbeardsley$ /Users/ianbeardsley/Desktop/object\ run ; exit;

If we use alphacentauri as the key to our model,
for modeling the future, then our task has been reduced,
through the work I have done, to quite a simple one.
growthrate=k=0.0621, objective=log 100/log e = 4.6 achievements,
Tzero=1969 when we landed on the moon, which at 2009 is 0.552=.0.12(4.6)
1/0.55 = 1.8=9/5 = R/r = Au/Ag, putting us in the age of gold:silver
Our equation is then, Time=(Object Achieved)/(Achievements/year)

How many simulations would you like to run (10 max)? 4
What is distance to object(0-4.6?) 4
What is the starting point (year) ?1969
Time to object=64.412239 years.
That is the year: 2033.412231

What is distance to object(0-4.6?) 0
What is the starting point (year) ?1969
Time to object=0.000000 years.
That is the year: 1969.000000

What is distance to object(0-4.6?) 4.6
What is the starting point (year) ?1969
Time to object=74.074074 years.
That is the year: 2043.074097

What is distance to object(0-4.6?) 4.5
What is the starting point (year) ?1969
Time to object=72.463768 years.
That is the year: 2041.463745

logout

[Process completed]

If we use alphacentauri as the key to our model,
for modeling the future, then our task has been reduced,
through the work I have done, to quite a simple one.
growthrate=k=0.0621, objective=log 100/log e = 4.6 achievements,
Tzero=1969 when we landed on the moon, which at 2009 is 0.552=.
0.12(4.6)
1/0.55 = 1.8=9/5 = R/r = Au/Ag, putting us in the age of
gold:silver
Our equation is then, Time=(Object Achieved)/(Achievements/year)

How many simulations would you like to run (10 max)? 2
What is distance to object(0-4.6?) 3.00
What is the starting point (year) ?1969
Time to object=48.309177 years.
That is the year: 2017.309204

What is distance to object(0-4.6?) 4.00
What is the starting point (year) ?1969
Time to object=64.412239 years.
That is the year: 2033.412231

All Output ⌄

Table 1

distance vs, year	distance	year				
0	0.00	0.00				
1	0.25	1973				
2	0.50	1977				
3	0.75	1981				
4	1.00	1985				
5	1.25	1989				
6	1.50	1993				
7	1.75	1997				
8	2.00	2001				
9	2.25	2005				

distance

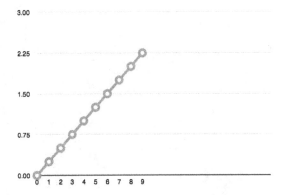

```
jharvard@appliance (~): cd Dropbox
jharvard@appliance (~/Dropbox): make input
clang -ggdb3 -O0 -std=c99 -Wall -Werror    input.c  -lcs50 -lm -o input
jharvard@appliance (~/Dropbox): ./input
```

Sierra Waters
The Brain
Enter Last Name: Waters
Enter First Name: Sierra
Enter Name: Brain
Enter Definite Article: The
Waters, Sierra: She was handed the newly discovered document in 2042.
Brain, The: He designed hyperdrive in 2044.
Between 2042 and 2044 is 2043.

If we use alphacentauri as the key to our model,
for modeling the future, then our task has been reduced,
through the work I have done, to quite a simple one.
growthrate=k=0.0621, objective=log 100/log e = 4.6 achievements,
Tzero=1969 when we landed on the moon, which at 2009 is 0.552=.0.12(4.6)
1/0.55 = 1.8=9/5 = R/r = Au/Ag, putting us in the age of gold:silver
Our equation is then, Time=(Object Achieved)/(Achievements/year)

How many simulations would you like to run (10 max)? 2
What is percent development towards objective(0-100)? 100
What is the starting point (year:enter 1969) ?1969
Time to object=74.165016 years.
That is the year: 2043.165039
What is percent development towards objective(0-100)? 7.4
What is the starting point (year:enter 1969) ?1969
Time to object=32.233292 years.
That is the year: 2001.233276

If you chose tzero as moon landing (1969), then you found
obect acheived 2043 between Sierra Waters and The Brain.
That time being reached in 74 years after time zero.
If you ran a second simulation again with t zero at 1969, and
ran the program for the 74 years to hyperdrive reduced by
a factor of ten (that is input 7.4 percent development.)
Then, you found object achieved in 2001, the year of Kubrick's
Starchild

jharvard@appliance (~/Dropbox):
```
```

```
jharvard@appliance (~): cd Dropbox
jharvard@appliance (~/Dropbox): ./objective
```

If we use alphacentauri as the key to our model,
for modeling the future, then our task has been reduced,
through the work I have done, to quite a simple one.
growthrate=k=0.0621, objective=log 100/log e = 4.6 achievements,
Tzero=1969 when we landed on the moon, which at 2009 is 0.552=.0.12(4.6)
1/0.55 = 1.8=9/5 = R/r = Au/Ag, putting us in the age of gold:silver
Our equation is then, Time=(Object Achieved)/(Achievements/year)

How many simulations would you like to run (10 max)? 8
What is percent develpment towards objective(0-100)? 15
What is the starting point (year:enter 1969) ?1969
Time to object=43.612415 years.
That is the year: 2012.612427

What is percent develpment towards objective(0-100)? 30
What is the starting point (year:enter 1969) ?1969
Time to object=54.775364 years.
That is the year: 2023.775391

What is percent develpment towards objective(0-100)? 45
What is the starting point (year:enter 1969) ?1969
Time to object=61.305267 years.
That is the year: 2030.305298

What is percent develpment towards objective(0-100)? 60
What is the starting point (year:enter 1969) ?1969
Time to object=65.938309 years.
That is the year: 2034.938354

What is percent develpment towards objective(0-100)? 75
What is the starting point (year:enter 1969) ?1969
Time to object=69.531982 years.
That is the year: 2038.531982

What is percent develpment towards objective(0-100)? 90
What is the starting point (year:enter 1969) ?1969
Time to object=72.468216 years.
That is the year: 2041.468262

What is percent develpment towards objective(0-100)? 100
What is the starting point (year:enter 1969) ?1969
Time to object=74.165016 years.
That is the year: 2043.165039

Table 1

time with %	percent	year
	15	12
	30	23
	45	30
	60	34
	75	38
	90	41

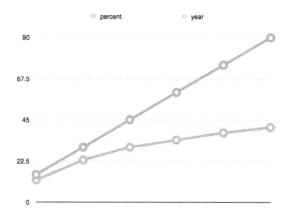

We see as percent progress (blue) climbs steady, the time to do it becomes less and less.

```
jharvard@appliance (~): cd Dropbox
jharvard@appliance (~/Dropbox): make modelfuture
clang -ggdb3 -O0 -std=c99 -Wall -Werror   modelfuture.c  -lcs50 -lm -o modelfuture
jharvard@appliance (~/Dropbox): ./modelfuture
```

$(p^{n1})(q^{n2})[W=N!/(n1!)(n2!)]$

$x=e^{(c*t)}$

W is the probability of landing on the star in N jumps.

N=n1+n2, n1=number of one light year jumps left,

n2=number of one light year jumps right.

What is 1, the nearest whole number of light years to the star, and

2, what is the star's name?

Enter 1: 4

Enter 2: alphacentauri

Star name: alphacentauri

Distance: 4

What is n1? 3

What is n2? 7

Since N=n1+n2, N=10

What is the probability, p(u), of jumping to the left? 1

What is the probability, p(v), of jumpint to the left? 2

What is the probability, q(y), of jumping to the right? 1

What is the probability, q(z), of jumping to the right? 2

p=u:v

q=y:z

N factorial = 1.000000

N factorial = 2.000000

N factorial = 6.000000

N factorial = 24.000000

N factorial = 120.000000

N factorial = 720.000000

N factorial = 5040.000000

N factorial = 40320.000000

N factorial = 362880.000000

N factorial = 3628800.000000

n1 factorial = 1.000000

n1 factorial = 2.000000

n1 factorial = 6.000000

n2 factorial = 1.000000

W=59062.500000 percent

W=59063.00 percent rounded to nearest integral

n2 factorial = 2.000000

W=29531.250000 percent

W=29531.00 percent rounded to nearest integral

n2 factorial = 6.000000

W=9843.750000 percent

W=9844.00 percent rounded to nearest integral

n2 factorial = 24.000000
W=2460.937500 percent
W=2461.00 percent rounded to nearest integral
n2 factorial = 120.000000
W=492.187500 percent
W=492.00 percent rounded to nearest integral
n2 factorial = 720.000000
W=82.031250 percent
W=82.00 percent rounded to nearest integral
n2 factorial = 5040.000000
W=11.718750 percent
W=12.00 percent rounded to nearest integral
What is t in years, the time over which the growth occurs? 40
log(W)=1.079181
loga/t=0.026980
growthrate constant=0.062136
log 100 = 2, log e = 0.4342, therfore
T=2/[(0.4342)(growthrate)]
T=74.13 years
What was the begin year for the period of growth? 1969
Object achieved in 2043.13
jharvard@appliance (~/Dropbox):

The Program In Python

```python
import math
object=float(raw_input("Enter percent development towards objective:
"));
Tzero=float(raw_input("Enter the starting point (enter 1969): "));
L=math.log10(object)/math.log10(2.718);
T=L/(0.0621);
Time=Tzero+T;
print("Time to objective is: " + str(T) + "years");
print("That is the year: " + str(Time));
```

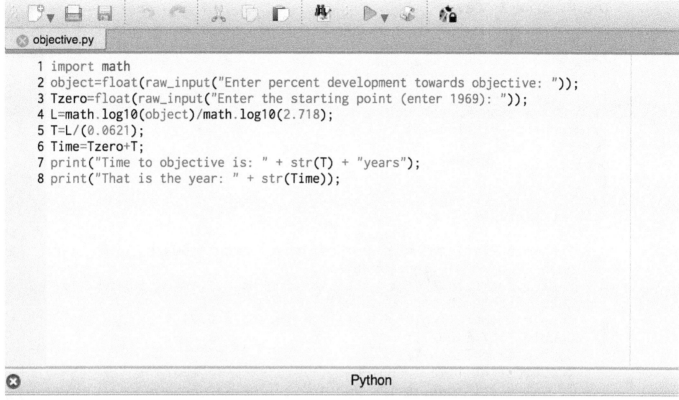

```
1 import math
2 object=float(raw_input("Enter percent development towards objective: "));
3 Tzero=float(raw_input("Enter the starting point (enter 1969): "));
4 L=math.log10(object)/math.log10(2.718);
5 T=L/(0.0621);
6 Time=Tzero+T;
7 print("Time to objective is: " + str(T) + "years");
8 print("That is the year: " + str(Time));
```

Python

```
Welcome to Canopy's interactive data-analysis environment!
 with pylab-backend set to: qt
Type '?' for more information.

In [1]: %run "/Users/ianbeardsley/Desktop/objective.py"

Enter percent development towards objective: 100

Enter the starting point (enter 1969): 1969
Time to objective is: 74.1650196331years
That is the year: 2043.16501963

In [2]: %run "/Users/ianbeardsley/Desktop/objective.py"

Enter percent development towards objective: 50

Enter the starting point (enter 1969): 1969
Time to objective is: 63.0020718638years
That is the year: 2032.00207186

In [3]:
```

The Program In Java

```java
import comp102x.IO;
/**
 * We model the human trajectory.
 *
 * @author (Ian Beardsley)
 * @version (version 01)
 */
public class objective
{

  public static void object()
  {
    System.out.print("Enter percent development towards objective: ");
    double object=IO.inputDouble();
    System.out.print("Enter the starting point (enter 1969): ");
    double Tzero=IO.inputDouble();
    double L=(Math.log10(object))/(Math.log10(2.718));
    double T=L/(0.0621);
    double Time=Tzero+T;
    IO.outputln("Time to objective is: " + T + "years");
    IO.outputln("That is the year: " + Time );
  }
}
```

```
BlueJ: Terminal Window - COMP 102x Lab 02

Enter percent development towards objective: 25
Enter the starting point (enter 1969): 1969
Time to objective is: 51.83912409451816years
That is the year: 2020.8391240945182
Enter percent development towards objective: 100
Enter the starting point (enter 1969): 1969
Time to objective is: 74.16501963308473years
That is the year: 2043.1650196330847
Enter percent development towards objective: 75
Enter the starting point (enter 1969): 1969
Time to objective is: 69.53197770634105years
That is the year: 2038.531977706341
```

Here we run the program in Java:

If we are to have any method for determining p and q, probabilities away from and, towards success, we have to consider the chief elements that whose state need to be assessed. The number one thing to consider is climate. Thus we present a comprehensive theory of climate:

Yes ◇

```
for modeling the future, then our task has been
reduced,
through the work I have done, to quite a simple one.
growthrate=k=0.0621, objective=log 100/log e = 4.6
achievements,
Tzero=1969 when we landed on the moon, which at 2009
is 0.552=.0.12(4.6)
1/0.55 = 1.8=9/5 = R/r = Au/Ag, putting us in the age
of gold:silver
Our equation is then, Time=(Object Achieved)/
(Achievements/year)

How many simulations would you like to run (10 max)?
4
What is percent develpment towards objective(0-100)?
40
What is the starting point (year:enter 1969) ?1969
Time to object=59.408405 years.
That is the year: 2028.408447

What is percent develpment towards objective(0-100)?
85
What is the starting point (year:enter 1969) ?1984
Time to object=71.547699 years.
That is the year: 2055.547607

What is percent develpment towards objective(0-100)?
100
What is the starting point (year:enter 1969) ?1990
Time to object=74.165016 years.
That is the year: 2064.165039

What is percent develpment towards objective(0-100)?
90
What is the starting point (year:enter 1969) ?1990
Time to object=72.468216 years.
That is the year: 2062.468262
```

space odyssey novels

```
Last login: Mon Apr 11 03:58:33 on ttys000
Claires-MBP:~ ianbeardsley$ /Users/ianbeardsley/Desktop/The\ Anomaly/
projectfuture\ copy ; exit;

If we use alphacentauri as the key to our model,
for modeling the future, then our task has been reduced,
through the work I have done, to quite a simple one.
growthrate=k=0.0621, objective=log 100/log e = 4.6 achievements,
Tzero=1969 when we landed on the moon, which at 2009 is 0.552=.
0.12(4.6)
1/0.55 = 1.8=9/5 = R/r = Au/Ag, putting us in the age of gold:silver
Our equation is then, Time=(Object Achieved)/(Achievements/year)

How many simulations would you like to run (10 max)? 5
What is percent develpment towards objective(0-100)? 7.4
What is the starting point (year:enter 1969) ?1969
Time to object=32.233292 years.
That is the year: 2001.233276
```

novel 1   humans hand on moon

```
What is percent develpment towards objective(0-100)? 84
What is the starting point (year:enter 1969) ?1990
Time to object=71.357109 years.
That is the year: 2061.357178
```

novel 3   graduated high school

```
What is percent develpment towards objective(0-100)? 100
What is the starting point (year:enter 1969) ?2927
Time to object=74.165016 years.
That is the year: 3001.165039
```

novel 4 (conclusion)

```
What is percent develpment towards objective(0-100)? 50
What is the starting point (year:enter 1969) ?2001
Time to object=63.002071 years.
That is the year: 2064.001953

What is percent develpment towards objective(0-100)? 45
What is the starting point (year:enter 1969) ?2001
Time to object=61.305267 years.
That is the year: 2062.305176

logout

[Process completed]
```

```
Last login: Mon Apr 11 04:05:45 on ttys000
Claires-MBP:~ ianbeardsley$ /Users/ianbeardsley/Desktop/The\ Anomaly/
projectfuture\ copy ; exit;

If we use alphacentauri as the key to our model,
for modeling the future, then our task has been reduced,
through the work I have done, to quite a simple one.
growthrate=k=0.0621, objective=log 100/log e = 4.6 achievements,
Tzero=1969 when we landed on the moon, which at 2009 is 0.552=.
0.12(4.6)
1/0.55 = 1.8=9/5 = R/r = Au/Ag, putting us in the age of gold:silver
Our equation is then, Time=(Object Achieved)/(Achievements/year)

How many simulations would you like to run (10 max)? 3
What is percent develpment towards objective(0-100)? 2
What is the starting point (year:enter 1969) ?2001
Time to object=11.162948 years.
That is the year: 2012.162964       mayan calendar

What is percent develpment towards objective(0-100)? 1.8
What is the starting point (year:enter 1969) ?2001
Time to object=9.466145 years.
That is the year: 2010.466187       novel 2

What is percent develpment towards objective(0-100)?
```

Table 1

objective	time	development X 10			
	1	74			
	10	18			
	61	840			
	1001	1000			

○ time   ○ development X 10

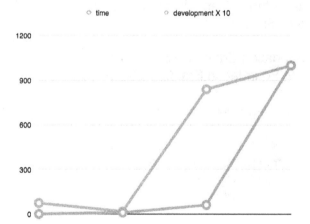

The Robot Series, The Foundation Series, and The Empire Series of Isaac Asimov are really one story. Because it begins with The Robot Series, where some humans have left earth for the nearby stars, The Spacers, as they are called, and because the Earth detective is called upon to solve a mystery on one of these outer worlds, he becomes respected by them, and ultimately through the engineering of a robot, he is maneuvered into leading a second wave of settling the this time the distant stars, Elijah Bailey becomes the one who leads to the human settlement of the Galaxy and, although dates are given at this point in the Foundation Novels by a fictional Galactic Calendar, we know when it started, because the earth calendar we use was used by him. Careful reading of the novels allows when one to figure out a galactic timeline for the history of the galaxy as was computed and is available online. This allows me to use my computer programs I wrote, to model the Asimovian Trajectory. Because Galactic Era and Foundation Era maintain the Earth year duration closely (The people not knowing its origins), we can calculate G.E. and F.E. dates for their Christ Era Equivalents.

We begin where we left off, with the intersection of the Sierra Waters of Paul Levinson (The Plot to Save Socrates) , and the computer called The Brain of Isaac Asimov (I, Robot).

1) (2042-2044) Sierra Waters handed newly discovered Ancient Greek Manuscript (2042). Ian Beardsley predicts hyperdrive for 2043 applying mathematics to the nearest star system. The Brain, in I, Robot, invents hyperdrive in 2044.
2) 3500 C.E. Spacetown, Earth; Elijah Bailey works with robot R. Daneel Olivaw to solve murder mystery, in The Caves of Steel, by Isaac Asimov.
3) (3505) Second wave of immigration from Earth led by Ben Bailey. Tensions arise between Spacer Worlds and Settler Worlds.
4) (12000 C.E) At center of Galaxy Trantor forms Republic of five worlds and the origins of humans are forgotten (The Currents of Space).
5) 12,500 C.E. is 1 G.E.
6) (12,067 Galactic Era or G.E. and Foundation Era or 1 F.E.) Puts 1 F.E. at about 12500+12067=24,567 C.E. = 1 F.E. or Foundation Era. Galactic Empire then lasted about 24,567-12.500=12,67 years.
7) (12500 C.E. or 1 G.E.: Galactic Era) Trantor becomes the seat of the Galactic Empire. (Read The Currents of Space).
8) (3 F.E.:Foundation Era) Hari Seldon who created the foundation on Terminus, dies.
9) (300 F.E.) The Mule, a mutant with mental powers overthrows the Foundation. This is 300 FE + 24,567 CE = 24,867 years after Christ Era (CE).
10) (310 F.E.) The Mule is defeated and The Foundation is restored democratic rule over the galaxy.
11) (498 F.E.) Golan Trevize choses the Gaia Model for the Galaxy, over The Foundation.) 498 +24,567 = 25,065 CE.

We have:

Sierra Waters and the Brain: 2043
Earth visits spacers (Elijah Bailey): 3500
Second Wave of Emigration (The Settlers): 3505
Trantor forms republic: 12,000
Trantor become seat of the galaxy: 12,500
Foundation Era: 24,570
The Mule: 24,867
Gaia is established: 25,065

The online timeline is much more detailed, but, from having read all the novels, I was able to choose out of it the major events a transitions leading to the ideal galactic society, called Gaia. Let us now make a graph that shows the rate at which humanity progresses towards this Gaia:

Table 1

event	CE					
sierra waters	2043					
spacers	3500					
settlers	3505					
trantor	12500					
foundation	24570					
the mule	24867					
gaia	25065					

CE

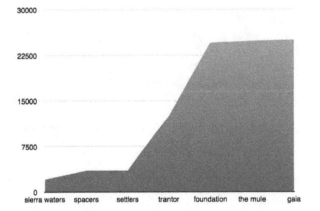

R = Solar Radius
r= lunar orbital radius
Au = gold
Ag = silver

R/r = Au/Ag = 9/5

(9/5)(4) = 7.2
Mars = 4
The earth precesses through one degree in 72 years
0.72 = Venus orbital radius in Astronomical Units (AU)

harmonic mean: Ga; As = 72.23
geometric mean: Ga; As = 72.27
23=Manuel Number
27=Manuel Number

23X27=621=L=Levinson's Number

Ga=69.72
As=74.92
Ga=Gallium
As=Arsenic

Ga and As are doping agents for making diodes, transistors, integrated circuitry,...the operational components of AI.

a) 2(69.72)(74.92)=10446.8448
b) (69.72)+(74.92)=144.64
c) a/b=72.2265~72.23
d) (69.72)(74.92)=5223.4224
e) sqrt(5223.4224)=72.27324816

9/5 connects pi to phi: 3.141+1.618=4.759
7=(9+5)/2

360/5=72 360-72=288
288/360 = 8/10 (8/10)+1 = 9/5

360/6 = 60 360-60-60=240
240/360 = 2/3 (2/3)+1 = 5/3

360/6=60 360-60 = 300
300/360 = 5/6 (5/6)+1 = 11/6

9/5, 5/3, 11/6

9/5: 5, 14, 23, 32,…
    1.8, 3.6, 5.4, 7.2,…

5/3: 8, 13, 18, 23,…
    1.7, 3.3, 5, 6.7

11/6: 6, 17, 28, 39
    11/6, 11/3, 11/2, 22/3

9/5: $a_n = 7.2n - 4$
5/3: $a_n = 3.3n + 3$
11/6: $a_n = 9n - 5$

=> <5/36, -10/33, -1/9> (Here we have inverted the coefficients of the equation of the plane)

$\sqrt{(5/36)^2 + (20/33)^2}$ = 0.0621 = Levinson's number~phi=0.618~0.62

Here we have eliminated n and taken the gradient to find the normal to the plane. The figure in the square root is the right ascension vector pointing to the constellation Aquila.

$\sin 45 = \frac{\sqrt{2}}{2}$
$\frac{\sqrt{2}}{2} = M$ = manuel's number

621=L= levinson's number

ML=440
440=standard concert pitch

23, 27 = Manuel Numbers
23X27=621=L

0.0621, Levinson's number is a growth rate for progress, There are 0.621 miles in a kilometer (km) and 1 km=1/10,000 of the distance from the pole to the equator. 0.0621 is the novelty rating in the McKenna Timewave for the year humans first set foot on the moon.

```
jharvard@appliance (~): cd Dropbox
jharvard@appliance (~/Dropbox): ./modelfuture

(p^n1)(q^n2)[W=N!/(n1!)(n2!)]
x=e^(c*t)
W is the probability of landing on the star in N jumps.
N=n1+n2, n1=number of one light year jumps left,
n2=number of one light year jumps right.
What is 1, the nearest whole number of light years to the star, and
2, what is the star's name?
Enter 1: 6
Enter 2: Barnard's
Star name: Barnard's
Distance: 6
What is n1? 1
What is n2? 7
Since N=n1+n2, N=8
What is the probability, p(u), of jumping to the left? 1
What is the probability, p(v), of jumpint to the left? 2
What is the probability, q(y), of jumping to the right? 1
What is the probability, q(z), of jumping to the right? 2
p=u:v
q=y:z
N factorial = 1.000000
N factorial = 2.000000
N factorial = 6.000000
N factorial = 24.000000
N factorial = 120.000000
N factorial = 720.000000
N factorial = 5040.000000
N factorial = 40320.000000
n1 factorial = 1.000000
n2 factorial = 1.000000
W=15750.000000 percent
W=15750.00 percent rounded to nearest integral
n2 factorial = 2.000000
W=7875.000000 percent
W=7875.00 percent rounded to nearest integral
n2 factorial = 6.000000
W=2625.000000 percent
W=2625.00 percent rounded to nearest integral
n2 factorial = 24.000000
W=656.250000 percent
W=656.00 percent rounded to nearest integral
n2 factorial = 120.000000
W=131.250000 percent
W=131.00 percent rounded to nearest integral
```

n2 factorial = 720.000000
W=21.875000 percent
W=22.00 percent rounded to nearest integral
n2 factorial = 5040.000000
W=3.125000 percent
W=3.00 percent rounded to nearest integral
What is t in years, the time over which the growth occurs? 40
log(W)=0.477121
loga/t=0.011928
growthrate constant=0.027471
log 100 = 2, log e = 0.4342, therfore
T=2/[(0.4342)(growthrate)]
T=167.67 years
What was the begin year for the period of growth? 1969
Object achieved in 2136.67
jharvard@appliance (~/Dropbox):

Unfortunately I can not run projections for Tau Bootes because my computer can not handle 100 factorial. It returns infinite. I could handle Barnard's Star just fine, but the best star in my mind was the original I used, Alpha Centauri, for projecting the future. When a star is both the same spectral class as the sun, and the closest star to you, you know it was made for the job! Nonetheless, to hand something like Tau Bootes, I would need a more powerful computer. Here are the runs of the programs for Barnard's Star, and Tau Bootes:

```
jharvard@appliance (~): cd Dropbox
jharvard@appliance (~/Dropbox): ./modelfuture

(p^n1)(q^n2)[W=N!/(n1!)(n2!)]
x=e^(c*t)
W is the probability of landing on the star in N jumps.
N=n1+n2, n1=number of one light year jumps left,
n2=number of one light year jumps right.
What is 1, the nearest whole number of light years to the star, and
2, what is the star's name?
Enter 1: 50
Enter 2: taubootes
Star name: taubootes
Distance: 50
What is n1? 25
What is n2? 75
Since N=n1+n2, N=100
What is the probability, p(u), of jumping to the left? 1
What is the probability, p(v), of jumpint to the left? 2
What is the probability, q(y), of jumping to the right? 1
What is the probability, q(z), of jumping to the right? 2
p=u:v
q=y:z
N factorial = 1.000000
N factorial = 2.000000
N factorial = 6.000000
N factorial = 24.000000
N factorial = 120.000000
N factorial = 720.000000
N factorial = 5040.000000
N factorial = 40320.000000
N factorial = 362880.000000
N factorial = 3628800.000000
N factorial = 39916800.000000
N factorial = 479001600.000000
N factorial = 6227020800.000000
N factorial = 87178289152.000000
N factorial = 1307674279936.000000
N factorial = 20922788478976.000000
N factorial = 355687414628352.000000
N factorial = 6402373530419200.000000
N factorial = 121645096004222976.000000
N factorial = 2432902023163674624.000000
N factorial = 51090940837169725440.000000
N factorial = 1124000724806013026304.000000
N factorial = 25852017444594485559296.000000
N factorial = 620448454699064672387072.000000
```

N factorial = 1551121107924624065796056.000000
N factorial = 40329149958961730317561216.000000
N factorial = 108888704151326908909019463688.000000
N factorial = 30488837162371534494525449830304.000000
N factorial = 8841763079319199070696741273600.000000
N factorial = 2652528899617243579828318744084448.000000
N factorial = 82228396855275206666381220831559688.000000
N factorial = 263130869936880661332419906660990976.000000
N factorial = 8683318509846655538309012935952826368.000000
N factorial = 295232829966533287161359432338880069632.000000
N factorial = inf
N factorial = inf
N factorial = inf
N factorial = inf

Running Bioplanet

Ian Beardsley

Climate Defined: Climate is the statistics of the weather including not just the average weather, but also the statistics of its variability, commonly calculated over periods of a year or more. The progression of seasons is not considered an example of climate variability. Separating signal from the noise is separating climate from the weather. That is we can say it will be warmer in the summer than in the winter, but we can't forecast the weather for any particular day.

Climate is determined by (1) the energy balance between incoming solar radiation and outgoing infrared radiation. That balance is affected by greenhouse gases, or the composition of the atmosphere, in other words. (2) atmospheric and oceanic convection, the flow or transfer of heat within various substances like, water (the ocean) or gases (the atmosphere). (3) Looking at climate change through geologic time, as a record of climate is embedded in the geological record, the substances that were in the atmosphere during an ice age in other words are recorded in the strata, which can be dated, so we can use this information to model where the climate is going.

Climate Cycles

Five billion years ago, when the earth and sun formed, the sun was much cooler than it is today, with an output of about 0.7 of its present output. Yet we know that water existed on the earth in liquid form, when it should have been ice. This is known as the Faint Young Star Paradox; the Earth should have been frozen up to 2.5 billion years ago.

Five hundred and fifty million years ago the Earth went through climate swings, being a snowball and then free of ice. Snowball Earth can be accounted for by positive feedback. Albedo is the percent of incoming radiation that is reflected into space. Snow has a higher albedo, so glaciation, or increased snow, increases the albedo of the earth making it emit more radiation back into a space making it cooler which, in turn, makes more snow, which increases the albedo still more, until you get a runaway icehouse, or Snowball Earth.

Fifty million years ago the earth reached its thermal maximum (Paleocene-Eocene). It took 20,000 years to develop, and 100,000 years to go away. The earth is cooling from that thermal maximum 50 million years ago.

For the past three million years glacial cycles have been going on with a periodicity of about 20,000 to 100,000 years. They are due to orbital dynamics of the earth. They are the glacial-interglacial cycles caused by eccentricity of the Earth orbit, which is a cycle of one hundred thousand years, the obliquity of the earth or change in tilt which is a cycle of 41 thousand years, and precession or wobble of the earth's spin, which has a cycle of 22 thousand years. The story of the earth has been a story of freezing over for 100,000 years, then briefly warming. We have been in one of these short warm periods for the past 10,000 years, called the Holocene, and it would seem it is responsible for the beginning of civilization 7,000 years ago. The last ice cover was about 18,000 years ago.

Composition Of The Atmosphere Through Time

The early Earth Atmosphere was probably predominantly hydrogen and helium (H2, He) but was lost to space. The later atmosphere was due to volcanic emissions, and impact by comets and meteorites (H20, CO2, SO2, CO, S2, Cl2, N2, H2, NH3, CH4). Oxygen came later as a by-product of living organisms. The origin of CO2 was volcanic emissions. It was absorbed by water forming carbonic acid, was deposited in the soil, then underwent reactions to become calcium carbonate:

$$H_2O + CO_2 \rightarrow H_2CO_3 (soil)$$
$$H_2CO_3 + CaSiO_3 \rightarrow CaCO_3 + SiO_2 + H_2O$$

Lifetime of substances in the atmosphere is given by:

Abundance (Gton)/Emissions (Gtons/year) = Lifetime (yr)

CO_2 has a lifetime in the atmosphere of 100 years. CO_2 exists in vegitation, soils, oceans, atmosphere and sediments. Lifetime relies in the simple model above relies on abundance and emissions are constant, that they are equilibrium processes.

Structure Of The Atmosphere

Divided by vertical gradient of temperature, there are four layers to the Earth Atmosphere:

Troposphere at 10-18 kilometers, Stratosphere ending at 50 kilometers, Mesosphere ending at 85 kilometers, then the Thermosphere.

80% of the mass is in the troposphere. In climate science we deal mostly with the troposphere, and a little with the stratosphere.

Heat Distribution Over The Earth, where heat is gained, where heat is lost.

Most of the warming is in the continents, Africa, South America, Canada, Asia. We should see a cooling of the lower stratosphere when we have a warming of the lower troposphere as a part of radiative balance of the planet. Raising the temperature one degree centigrade of a cubic meter of sea water requires 4,000 times more energy input than to raise a cubic meter of atmosphere one degree. Water has a high specific heat, that is it takes one calorie to raise a gram of it one degree centigrade. That is one factor that keeps the Earth from getting too warm. The vast majority of change in the energy climate system has gone into the ocean, mostly into the upper 700 meters. Water expands when you increase its temperature, like most substances, and the sea rise we are seeing is in part due to that. But most is due to the melting of land ice. Most of the land mass in the Northern Hemisphere, so, in the spring, when there is a lot of plant growth in the Northern Hemisphere, there is a drop in CO_2. Annually, anthropogenic emissions increase CO_2 by about nine gigatons or 900 terragrams. This is only about 1% of the burden, but it must be remembered that is annual and increases with time.

Precipitation is the product of condensation of water vapor that falls under gravity, like rain, sleet, snow, hail,...

Most of the CO_2 is absorbed by the ocean and the decrease its PH, making it more acidic. What are the effects on the corral reefs and plankton?

The temperature is pretty much constant in the tropics throughout the year. Prevalence of ocean in the southern hemisphere keeps that area relatively stable.

During the spring and summer foliage comes out and absorbs CO_2, then when leaves fall, and decay, that CO_2 is returned to the atmosphere in the Fall. Most cooling is in evaporation of water, especially in the tropics. Radiation is absorbed in the tropics and emitted in the poles. The Ocean and the atmosphere transport absorption in the tropics to the poles, where it is emitted. The tropics absorb more radiation than they emit and the poles emit more radiation than they receive.

Albedo

Albedo is a function of surface reflectivity and atmospheric reflectivity. Atmospheric albedo seems to play the primary role in the overall albedo of a planet. Albedo is the percent of light incident to a surface that is reflected back into space. It has a value ranging from zero to one inclusive. Zero is a black surface absorbing all incident light and one is a white surface reflecting all incident light back into space. Albedo plays a dominant role in the climate of a planet. Let us see if we can find a relationship between composition of a planet and its albedo if not in its distance from the star it orbits and its albedo, even a relationship between its albedo and orbital number, in that albedo could be a function of distance from the star a planet orbits because composition seems to be a function of distance of a planet from the star it orbits. As in the inner planets are solid, or terrestrial, and the outer planets are gas giants. There may be an analogue to the Titius-Bode rule for planetary distribution, but for albedo with respect to planetary number. The inner planets are dominantly CO_2, Nitrogen, Oxygen, and water vapor, the outer planets, hydrogen and helium.

1. Mercury albedo of 0.06 composition 95% CO_2
2. Venus albedo of 0.75 composition clouds of sulfuric acid
3. Earth albedo of 0.30 composition Nitrogen, Oxygen, H_2O or water vapor
4. Mars albedo of 0.29 composition CO_2
5. Asteroids
6. Jupiter albedo of 0.53 composition hydrogen and helium
7. Saturn albedo of 0.47 composition hydrogen and helium
8. Uranus albedo of 0.51 composition hydrogen, helium, methane
9. Neptune albedo of 0.41 composition of hydrogen and helium

We see the outer gas giant, which are composed chiefly of hydrogen and helium have albedos around 50%. Earth and Mars, the two planets in the habitable zone, are about the same (30%).

Go to the next page for a graph of albedo to planetary number.

mercury	0.06
venus	0.75
earth	0.3
mars	0.29
asteroids	
jupiter	0.52
saturn	0.47
uranus	0.51
neptune	0.41

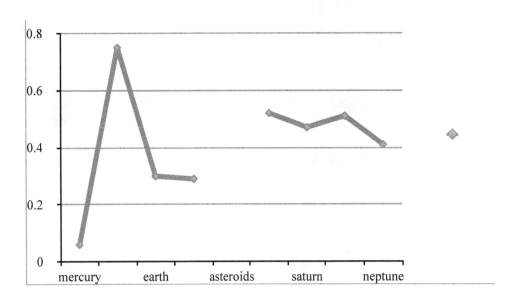

The average for the albedo of the inner planets is:
(0.06+0.75+0.3+0.29)/4 = 0.35
This is close to the albedo of the habitable planets Earth and Mars.

The average for the albedo of the outer planets is:
(0.52+0.47+0.51+0.41)/4 + 0.4775 ~0.48
This says the outer planets are all close to 0.48~0.5

All this also says, if the planet is solid and habitable it probably has an albedo of around 0.3, otherwise it is an outer gaseous planet and probably has an albedo of around 0.5.

As climate science is a new science, there are many models for the climate and I learned my climate science at MIT in a free online edX course. One can generate a basic model for climate with nothing more than high school algebra using nothing more than the temperature of the sun, the distance of the earth from the sun, and the earth's albedo, the percent of light it reflects back into space.

The luminosity of the sun is:

$$L_0 = 3.9 \times 10^{26} \, J/s$$

The separation between the earth and the sun is:

$$1.5 \times 10^{11} \, m$$

The solar luminosity at the earth is reduced by the inverse square law, so the solar constant is:

$$S_0 = \frac{3.9 \times 10^{26}}{4\pi (1.5 \times 10^{11})^2} = 1,370 \, Watts/meter^2$$

That is the effective energy hitting the earth per second per square meter. This radiation is equal to the temperature, T_e, to the fourth power by the steffan-bolzmann constant, sigma (σ). T_e can be called the effective temperature, the temperature entering the earth.

S_0 intercepts the earth disc, πr^2, and distributes itself over the entire earth surface, $4\pi r^2$, while 30% is reflected back into space due to the earth's albedo, a, which is equal to 0.3, so

$$\sigma T_e^4 = \frac{S_0}{4}(1 - a)$$

$$(1 - a)S_0 \frac{\pi r^2}{4\pi r^2}$$

But, just as the same amount of radiation that enters the system, leaves it, to have radiative equilibrium, the atmosphere radiates back to the surface so that the radiation from the atmosphere, σT_a^4 plus the radiation entering the earth, σT_e^4 is the radiation at the surface of the earth, σT_s^4. However,

$$\sigma T_a^4 = \sigma T_e^4$$

and we have:

$$\sigma T_s^4 = \sigma T_a^4 + \sigma T_e^4 = 2\sigma T_e^4$$

$$T_s = 2^{\frac{1}{4}} T_e$$

$$\sigma T_e^4 = \frac{S_0}{4}(1-a)$$

$$\sigma = 5.67 \times 10^{-8}$$

$$S_0 = 1,370$$

$$a = 0.3$$

$$\frac{1,370}{4}(0.7) = 239.75$$

$$T_e^4 = \frac{239.75}{5.67 \times 10^{-8}} = 4.228 \times 10^9$$

$$T_e = 255 Kelvin$$

So, for the temperature at the surface of the Earth:

$$T_s = 2^{\frac{1}{4}} T_e = 1.189(255) = 303 Kelvin$$

Let's convert that to degrees centigrade:

Degrees Centigrade = 303 - 273 = 30 degrees centigrade

And, let's convert that to Fahrenheit:

Degrees Fahrenheit = 30(9/5)+32=86 Degrees Fahrenheit

In reality this is warmer than the average annual temperature at the surface of the earth, but, in this model, we only considered radiative heat transfer and not convective heat transfer. In other words, there is cooling due to vaporization of water (the formation of clouds) and due to the condensation of water vapor into rain droplets (precipitation or the formation of rain).

The incoming radiation from the sun is about 1370 watts per square meter as determined by the energy per second emitted by the sun reduced by the inverse square law at earth orbit. We calculate the total absorbed energy intercepted by the Earth's disc (pi)r^2, its distribution over its surface area 4(pi)r^2 and take into account that about 30% of that is reflected back into space, so the effective radiation hitting the Earth's surface is about 70% of the incoming radiation reduced by four. Radiative energy is equal to temperature to the fourth power by the Stefan-boltzmann constant. However, the effective incoming radiation is also trapped by greenhouse gases and emitted down towards the surface of the earth (as well as emitted up towards space from this lower atmosphere called the troposphere), the most powerful greenhouse gas being CO_2 (Carbon Dioxide) and most abundant and important is water vapour. This doubles the radiation warming the surface of the planet. The atmosphere is predominately Nitrogen gas (N_2) and Oxygen gas (O_2), about 95 percent. These gases, however, are not greenhouse gases. The greenhouse gas CO_2, though only exists in trace amounts, and water vapour, bring the temperature of the Earth up from minus 18 degrees centigrade (18 below freezing) to an observed average of plus 15 degrees centigrade (15 degrees above freezing). Without these crucial greenhouse gases, the Earth would be frozen. They have this enormous effect on warming the planet even with CO_2 existing only at 400 parts per million. It occurs naturally and makes life on Earth possible. However, too much of it and the Earth can be too warm, and we are now seeing amounts beyond the natural levels through anthropogenic sources, that are making the Earth warmer than is favorable for the conditions best for life to be maximally sustainable. We see this increase in CO_2 beginning with the industrial era. The sectors most responsible for the increase are power, industry, and transportation. Looking at records of CO_2 amounts we see that it was 315 parts per million in 1958 and rose to 390 parts per million in 2010. It rose above 40s in radiative equilibrium, that is, it loses as much radiation as it receives. Currently we are slightly out of radiative balance, the Earth absorbs about one watt per square meter more than it loses. That means its temperature is not steady, but increasing.

Equilibrium: The Crux of Climate Science

Let us say the Earth is cold, absolute zero, then suddenly the sun blinks on. The Earth will receive radiation and start to get warmer. As it gets warmer, it starts to lose some of the heat it receives, and warms slower and slower. There are various mechanisms by which the Earth can lose heat; which ones kick in and by how much they draw heat off the planet, are vary numerous and, vary in a wide spectrum as to the amount of heat, or energy in other words, that they can draw off the planet and, at what rates. We have discussed two mechanisms: radiative heat transfer, and convective heat transfer. An example is the vaporization of the ocean, which is water becoming a gas, or clouds in other words. The heat required to raise its temperature to the point that it vaporizes is one calorie per gram degree centigrade. This represents a loss of heat, or energy, from the sun, that would have gone into warming the planet. As well, when the vaporized water, or what are called clouds, condenses into liquid, this represents another loss of heat-energy that would have gone into warming the planet, for the same reason it takes energy to make a refrigerator cold. This condensation of water vapor to its liquid form, is called precipitation, the formation of water droplets, or what we commonly call rain. The amount of water that is vaporized from the ocean must equal the amount that precipitates, rains back upon the earth, in other words. If these two were not equal, then the oceans would dry up. Back to the warming earth: as it warms, it does so slower and slower as the cooling mechanisms kick in. Eventually the rate at which the earth warms will slow down to zero. At this point the amount of energy it receives equals the amount of energy it loses and the earth is at a constant temperature. This is called an *equilibrium state.* For the earth, this should be about 15 degrees centigrade in the annual average temperature. If the earth goes out of equilibrium, that is grows warmer or colder with time, then there can be a great deal of causes for this to happen, and many complex factors must be considered to calculate how long it will take the earth to return to a stable temperature (equilibrium state) and to determine what the temperature of the earth will be when it is back in equilibrium.

From a purely mathematical perspective, equilibrium states can be described by placing a ball in a dish and displacing it to either the left or right: it will roll back and forth until by friction it settles at the bottom of the dish motionless (in an equilibrium state). There can be two types of equilibrium states. One, like we just described, a valley, or two, the reverse: a peak where we have a ball balanced at the apex of a mountain. In this scenario, if I displace the ball to the left or right, it will go out of equilibrium, but never return to equilibrium, like it did in the previous example of a trough: but rather roll down the mountain, never to return.

The earth is currently out of equilibrium, that is, it receives more energy per second than it loses by one watt per square meter. This means the earth is warming. The reason for this is mostly because human activity is putting more CO_2 into the atmosphere than should be there, which means the earth retains more heat than it can lose.

Ian Beardsley
March 25, 2016

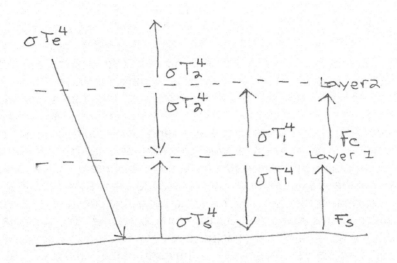

σT_e^4 : Radiation Entering

σT_s^4 : Radiation From Surface

σT_2^4 : Radiation From Layer 2

σT_1^4 : Radiation From Layer 1

F_s : Flux Convective from Surface

F_c : Flux Convective from Layer 1

Climate Modeling with Radiative Heat Transfer And Convection

$$T_1=T_2+\Delta T \quad Or \quad \Delta T=T_2-T_1 \quad T_s=T_2+2\Delta T \quad T_2=T_e \quad T_1=T_e+\Delta T$$

$$T_s=T_e+2\Delta T \qquad x\equiv\frac{\Delta T}{T_e} \qquad surface: \; F_s+\sigma T_s^4=\sigma T_e^4+\sigma T_1^4$$

$$layer \; 2: \; 2\sigma T_e^4=\sigma T_1^4+F_c \quad F_s+\sigma T_s^4-\sigma T_e^4=\sigma T_1^4 \quad 2\sigma T_e^4-F_c=\sigma T_1^4$$

$$F_s+\sigma T_s^4-\sigma T_e^4=2\sigma T_e^4-F_c \quad F_s+\sigma T_s^4=3\sigma T_e^4-F_c \quad \sigma T_s^4=3\sigma T_e^4-F_c$$

$$\sigma T_s^4=3\sigma T_e^4-F_c-F_s \qquad\qquad F_s=\sigma T_e^4+\sigma T_1^4-\sigma T_s^4 \quad F_c=2\sigma T_e^4-\sigma T_1^4$$

$$F_s=\sigma T_e^4[1+(1+x)^4-(1+2x)^4] \qquad F_c=\sigma T_e^4[2-(1+x)^4$$

$$\sigma T_s^4=3\sigma T_e^4-\sigma T_e^4[2-(1+x)^4]-\sigma T_e^4[1+(1+x)^4-(1+2x)^4]$$

$$Where: \; \sigma T_e^4=(1-a)\frac{S_0}{4} \quad \sigma=5.67\times10^{-8} \quad a=0.3 \; for \; earth$$

$$If \; \Delta T=0 \; Then \; x=0 \; and \; T_s=T_e$$

```
import comp102x.IO;
/**
 * Here we write a program in java that models the temperature of a planet for a star
 * of given luminosity.
 * @author (Ian Beardsley)
 * @version (Version 01 March 2016)
 */
public class bioplanet
{


    public static void bioplanet()
    {
        System.out.print("Enter the luminosity of the star in solar luminosities: ");
        double lum = IO.inputDouble();
        System.out.print("Enter the distance of the planet from the star in AU: ");
        double r=IO.inputDouble();
        System.out.print("Enter albedo of the planet (0-1): ");
        double a=IO.inputDouble();
        double R=(1.5E11)*r;
        double S=(3.9E26)*lum;
        double b=S/(4*3.141*R*R);
        double N = (1-a)*b/(4*(5.67E-8));
        double root = Math.sqrt(N);
        double number = Math.sqrt(root);
        double answer = 1.189*number;
        IO.outputln("The surface temperature of the planet is: "+answer+ " K");
        double C = answer - 273;
        double F = 1.8*C + 32;
        IO.outputln("That is: " +C+ " degrees centigrade");
        IO.outputln("Which is: " + F + " degrees Fahrenheit");


    }
}
```

Enter the luminosity of the star in solar luminosities: 1
Enter the distance of the planet from the star in AU: 1
Enter albedo of the planet (0-1): .3
The surface temperature of the planet is: 303.72751882043394 K
That is: 30.727518820433943 degrees centigrade
Which is: 87.3095338767811 degrees Fahrenheit

Run BioPlanet

Terminal Saved Output 01 (Climate Science by Ian Beardsley) Feb 17, 2016

Last login: Wed Feb 17 06:14:19 on ttys000
Claires-MBP:~ ianbeardsley$ /Users/ianbeardsley/Desktop/stelr/stellar ; exit;
We determine the surface temperature of a planet.
What is the luminosity of the star in solar luminosities? 2
What is the albedo of the planet (0-1)?.5
What is the distance from the star in AU? 1.4142135
The surface temperature of the planet is: 279.223602 K
That is 6.223602 C, or 43.202484 F
The luminosity of the star in joules per second is: 78.00E25
The habitable zone of the star in AU is: 1.414214
Flux at planet is 1.01 times that at earth.
That is 1379.60 Watts per square meter
logout

[Process completed]

According to my computer simulated program if a star is exactly twice as bright as the sun and
reflects 50% of the light received back into space, and is at a distance of square root of 2 AU
(AU = average earth-sun separation), then the flux at the planet is the same as that at earth and
the planet is exactly in the habitable zone. In this scenario, the average yearly temperature is a
cool six degrees celsius.

Let us run this program for other values:

Here we choose golden ratio=1.618 for amount of solar luminosities, the golden ratio conjugate
=0.618 AU for distance from star, and the same for albedo (percent of light reflected back into
space by the planet. It returns an average yearly temperature of approximately fahrenheit-
celsius equivalence, -40 degrees F = -40 degrees C:

Last login: Wed Feb 17 06:28:41 on ttys000
Claires-MBP:~ ianbeardsley$ /Users/ianbeardsley/Desktop/stelr/stellar ; exit;
We determine the surface temperature of a planet.
What is the luminosity of the star in solar luminosities? 1.618
What is the albedo of the planet (0-1)?0.618
What is the distance from the star in AU? 1.618
The surface temperature of the planet is: 231.462616 K
That is -41.537384 C, or -42.767292 F
The luminosity of the star in joules per second is: 63.10E25
The habitable zone of the star in AU is: 1.272006
Flux at planet is 0.62 times that at earth.
That is 852.66 Watts per square meter
logout

[Process completed]

Here is another interesting scenario. It returns yearly average temp, freezing temperature of water:

Last login: Wed Feb 17 06:40:34 on ttys000
Claires-MBP:~ ianbeardsley$ /Users/ianbeardsley/Desktop/stelr/stellar ; exit;
We determine the surface temperature of a planet.
What is the luminosity of the star in solar luminosities? 60
What is the albedo of the planet (0-1)?0.605
What is the distance from the star in AU? 7.2
The surface temperature of the planet is: 273.042633 K
That is 0.042633 C, or 32.076740 F
The luminosity of the star in joules per second is: 2340.00E25
The habitable zone of the star in AU is: 7.745966
Flux at planet is 1.17 times that at earth.
That is 1596.76 Watts per square meter
logout

[Process completed]

Now for one solar luminosity, albedo of golden ratio conjugate, earth-sun separation. It returns 15F. Earth average yearly temperature is 15C:

Last login: Wed Feb 17 06:41:43 on ttys000
Claires-MBP:~ ianbeardsley$ /Users/ianbeardsley/Desktop/stelr/stellar ; exit;
We determine the surface temperature of a planet.
What is the luminosity of the star in solar luminosities? 1
What is the albedo of the planet (0-1)?0.6
What is the distance from the star in AU? 1
The surface temperature of the planet is: 264.073395 K
That is -8.926605 C, or 15.932111 F
The luminosity of the star in joules per second is: 39.00E25
The habitable zone of the star in AU is: 1.000000
Flux at planet is 1.01 times that at earth.
That is 1379.60 Watts per square meter
logout

[Process completed]

Let us try a planet at mars orbit=1.523 AU with 10 solar luminosities albedo golden ratio
conjugate = phi=0.618. It returns about 100 degrees celsius, the boiling temperature of water:

Last login: Wed Feb 17 06:46:52 on ttys000
Claires-MBP:~ ianbeardsley$ /Users/ianbeardsley/Desktop/stelr/stellar ; exit;
We determine the surface temperature of a planet.
What is the luminosity of the star in solar luminosities? 10
What is the albedo of the planet (0-1)?0.618
What is the distance from the star in AU? 1.523
The surface temperature of the planet is: 376.162537 K
That is 103.162537 C, or 217.692566 F
The luminosity of the star in joules per second is: 390.00E25
The habitable zone of the star in AU is: 3.162278
Flux at planet is 4.34 times that at earth.
That is 5947.77 Watts per square meter
logout

[Process completed]

Run ModelPlanet

I fixed the bug in this program and it models the earth perfectly, exactly returning it mass. Here it is running it on the jharvard emulator:

jharvard@appliance (~): cd Dropbox
jharvard@appliance (~/Dropbox): make modelplanet
clang -ggdb3 -O0 -std=c99 -Wall -Werror   modelplanet.c -lcs50 -lm -o modelplanet
jharvard@appliance (~/Dropbox): ./modelplanet

We input the radii of the layers of a planet,...
and their corresponding densities,...
to determine the planet's composition.
Iron Core Density Fe=7.87 g/cm^3
Lithosphere Density Ni = 8.91 g/cm^3
Mantle Density Si=2.33 g/cm^3
Earth Radius = 6,371 km
Earth Mass = 5.972E24 Kg

what is r1, the radius of the core in km? 500
what is p1, its density in g/cm^3? 7.87
what is r2, outer edge of layer two in km? 5000
what is p2, density of layer two in g/cm^3? 8.91
what is r3, the radius of layer 3 in km? 6371
what is p3, density of layer three in g/cm^3? 2.33

r1=500.00, r2=5000.00, r3=6371.00, p1=7.87, p2=8.91, p3=2.33

the core has a mass of 0.04 E23 Kg
thickness of core is 500.00
layer two has a mass of 46.60 E23 Kg
layer two thickness is 4500.00
layer three has a mass of 13.04 E23 Kg
layer three thickness is 1371.00

the mass of the planet is 5.97 E24 Kg
jharvard@appliance (~/Dropbox):

Let's run it in the OS X utility terminal for a larger planet, say Jupiter sized:

The radius of Jupiter is 69, 911 km

density of iron is 7.87 gm/cm^3
density of methane is 0.7923 g/cm^3
density of helium is 0.1785
density of hydrogen 0.0899 g/cm^3

mass of jupiter: 1.89813 E27 kg

running the program:

Last login: Tue Mar 8 23:35:48 on ttys000
Claires-MBP:~ ianbeardsley$ /Users/ianbeardsley/Desktop/model\ planet\ bug\ fixed/model\
planet ; exit;

We input the radii of the layers of a planet,...
and their corresponding densities,...
to determine the planet's composition.
Iron Core Density Fe=7.87 g/cm^3
Lithosphere Density Ni = 8.91 g/cm^3
Mantle Density Si=2.33 g/cm^3
Earth Radius = 6,371 km
Earth Mass = 5.972E24 Kg

what is r1, the radius of the core in km? 10000
what is p1, its density in g/cm^3? 7.87
what is r2, outer edge of layer two in km? 30000
what is p2, density of layer two in g/cm^3? 0.7923
what is r3, the radius of layer 3 in km? 69911
what is p3, density of layer three in g/cm^3? 0.1785

r1=10000.00, r2=30000.00, r3=69911.00, p1=7.87, p2=0.79, p3=0.18

the core has a mass of 329.60 E23 Kg
thickness of core is 10000.00
layer two has a mass of 862.72 E23 Kg
layer two thickness is 20000.00
layer three has a mass of 2352.52 E23 Kg
layer three thickness is 39911.00

the mass of the planet is 354.48 E24 Kg

Run ModelOcean

Last login: Sat Mar 26 07:26:13 on ttys000
/Users/ianbeardsley/Desktop/Model\ Ocean\ 01/modelocean ; exit;
Claires-MBP:~ ianbeardsley$ /Users/ianbeardsley/Desktop/Model\ Ocean\ 01/modelocean ;
exit;

The surface area of the earth is 510E6 square km.
About three quarters of that is ocean.
Half the surface area of the earth is receiving sunlight at any given moment.
0.75*510E6/2 = 200E6 square km recieving light from the sun.
There is about one gram of water per cubic cm.

Is the section of water you are considering on the order of:
1 a waterhole
2 a pond
3 the ocean
1
How many square meters of water are warmed? 9
How many meters deep is the water warmed? 0.5
That is 4.500 cubic meters of water.
4.500 cubic meters of water has a mass of about 4500.000 E3 grams.

The specific heat of water is one gram per calorie-degree centigrade.
One calorie is 4.8400 Joules.
The light entering the earth is 1,370 Joules per second per square meter.
That is 1,370 watts per square meter.
By what percent is the light entering reduced by clouds? (0-1) 1
Incident radiation is: 1370.000 watts per square meter.

The body of water is exposed to the sunlight from 10:00 AM to 2:00 PM.
That is four hours which are 14,400 seconds.
How many square meters of water are to be considered? 9
How deep is the water heated (in meters)? 0.5
The volume of water in cubic meters is: 4.500
That is 4500.000 E3 cubic centimeters.
That is 4500.000 E3 grams of water in 4.500 cubic meters of water.
That is 4.500 cubic meters heated by 36684296.000 calories
What is the intitial temperature of the body of water? 68
The temperature of the body of water has increased; 0.120 degrees C.
That means the temperature of the body of water is: 68.120 degrees C.
logout

[Process completed]

Ian Beardsley

The Mystery In Our Units of Measurement

by

Ian Beardsley

Our units of measurement evolved out of a complex history. The mile, for example, evolved out of a rough estimate of the approximate time it took to walk a horse around a track of no precise length, in order to exercise it. A kilometer was defined in modern times as one ten thousandth of the distance from the pole of the earth to its equator. Yet it is a curious fact that there are 0.621 miles in a kilometer, which is close to the golden ratio (0.618). More interesting is that 0.621 multiplied with the square root of two over two is equal to A440, which is standard concert pitch, the cycles per second of the frequency the oboe sounds for the orchestra to tune all of its instruments to the same pitch before performing a work. I first began to discover how these randomly evolved units of measurement were connected to the Universe, Nature, and each other back around 2012. It all began with the observation:

R=solar radius
r=lunar orbital radius
Au=molar mass of gold
Ag=molar mass of silver

R/r = Au/Ag =9/5

Which lead to:

Five-fold Symmetry: The Biological

$$\frac{360}{5} = 72; 360 - 72 = 288; \frac{288}{360} = \frac{8}{10}; \frac{8}{10} + 1 = \frac{9}{5}$$

Six-fold Symmetry: The Physical

$$\frac{360}{6} = 60; 360 - 60 - 60 = 240; \frac{240}{360} = \frac{2}{3}; \frac{2}{3} + 1 = \frac{5}{3}$$

Alternate Six-fold: The Physical

$$\frac{360}{6} = 60; 360 - 60 = 300; \frac{300}{360} = \frac{5}{6}; \frac{5}{6} + 1 = \frac{11}{6}$$

9/5: 5, 14, 23, 32,... and 1.8, 3.6, 5.4, 7.2,...
$a_n = 7.2n - 4$

5/3: 8, 13, 18, 23,... and 1.7, 3.3, 5, 6.7,...
$a_n = 3.3n + 3$

11/6: 6, 17, 28, 39,.. and 11/6, 11/3, 11/2, 22/3,...

$\pi + \phi = 3.141 + 1.618 = 4.759; 7 = (5 + 9)/2$
$\pi + e = 3.141 + 2.718 = 5.859; 9/5 = 1.8$

This lead me to consider the following integral:

(v) = 3 + 3.3t

(v)=at=(33/10)t where v is velocity, a is acceleration, and t is time.

3=(33/10)t
(t) = 30/33

980 cm/s/s = g = the surface gravity of the earth to nearest 10

(980 cm/s/s)(3.3)=3,234 cm/s/s

(3,234 cm/s/s)(30/33 s) = 2,940 cm/s = v_0 v_0 is the initial velocity

Thus we can write the equation as:

(v) = 2,940 cm/s + (3,234 cm/s/s)t

This is the differential equation:

(dx) = (2,940 cm/s)dt + (3,234 cm/s/s)t dt

The only thing we lack in solving this is a time for which we can derive a distance. The Earth rotates through 15 degrees in one hour, so we consider 15 seconds. The result is

(x_0) = (2,940 cm/s)15 + ((1/2)(3,234) cm/s/s)15^2 = 44,100 +363,825 = 407925 cm

407925 cm/100/1000 = 4.07925 km

This is nearly four kilometers. If a kilometer is defined as one ten thousandth of the distance from the pole to the equator, then 4 kilometers is one ten thousandth the circumference of the Earth.

The Integral From 0 To 15 Seconds:

$$\int_0^{15} (2,940\, cm/s)\, dt + \int_0^{15} (3,234\, cm/s/s)t\, dt = 4.07925\, km$$

Thus we can write the equation as:

(v) = 2,940 cm/s + (3,234 cm/s/s)t

This is the differential equation:

(dx) = (2,940 cm/s)dt + (3,234 cm/s/s)t dt

Integral From 0 To 15 Seconds

$$\int_0^{15} (2,940\, cm/s)\, dt + \int_0^{15} (3,234\, cm/s/s)t\, dt = 4.07925\, km$$

Mach 1 = 768 mph =1,235 km/hour

That is mach 1 in dry air at 20 degrees C (68 degrees F, or room temperature) at sea level.

If we write, where 1,235 km/hr (mach 1) = 0.343 km/s, then:

34,300 cm/s =2,940 cm/s + (3234 cm/s/s)t

and

t=9.696969697 seconds = 9 23/33 s = 320/33 seconds ~ 9.7 seconds

So, the integral is a time of 9.7 seconds to reach mach 1. Putting that time in the integral:

(x) = (2,940)(320/33) + 1/2(3234(320/33)^2 = 180,557 cm 1.80557 km ~ 1.8km

Thus, with the integral we reach mach one in about 9.7 seconds after traveling a distance of 1.8 kilometers.

1.8=9/5=R/r=Au/Ag

I have taken upon myself to search for some basic unit of energy that is connected to Nature and The Universe. Here is how I have done it:

Electron Volt: A unit of energy equal to the work done on an electron in accelerating it through a potential of one volt. It is 1.6E10-19 Joules (Google Search Engine)

Volt: Potential energy that will impart on joule of energy per coulomb of charge that passes through it. (Wikipedia)

Coulomb: The charge of 6.242E18 protons or 6.242E18 electrons.

Forward Bias: A diode (silicon) must have 0.7 volts across it to turn it on, 0.3 volts (Germanium). This is called forward voltage. The forward voltage threshold is 0.6 volts.

(0.6 volts)(1.6E-19)=9.6E-20 Joules

This is the energy to turn on a diode, or the threshold of life for artificial intelligence.

Aerobic respiration requires oxygen (O_2) in order to generate ATP. Although carbohydrates, fats, and proteins are consumed as reactants, it is the preferred method of pyruvate breakdown in glycolysis and requires that pyruvate enter the mitochondria in order to be fully oxidized by the Krebs cycle. The products of this process are carbon dioxide and water, but the energy transferred is used to break strong bonds in ADP as the third phosphate group is added to form ATP (adenosine triphosphate), by substrate-level phosphorylation, NADH and FADH2

Simplified reaction:

$C_6H_{12}O_6$ (s) + 6 O_2 (g) → 6 CO_2 (g) + 6 H_2O (l) + heat
ΔG = –2880 kJ per mol of $C_6H_{12}O_6$

(From Wikipedia)

(2,880,000 J)/(6.02E23 C6H12O6) =4.784E-18 J = basic unit of biological life
(4.784E-18 J)/(9.6E-20 J)=49.8~50

This says the basic energy unit of organic, or biological life, is about 50 times greater than the basic energy unit of electronic life, or artificial intelligence.

That is 0.6(50)=30 electron volts = basic unit of energy for biological life.

So, we see the visible spectrum for one photon of light begins where the energy of the photon is 2 "bue" electronic which is 100 "bue" biological and that that photon has a wavelength of 1.0 micrometers.

This is all about vision in a robot or AI.

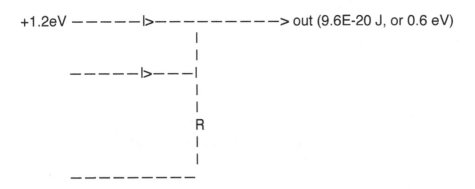

A photon has to have a minimum energy of 1.2 electron volts to impart to an electron for it to turn on the simplest of logic gates; a one on, one off, OR GATE, for there to be an output of one "bue" (basic unit of energy electronic) , which 9.6E-20 Joules, as I have calculated it.

Use Planck's Equation: $E=hv$ where $h= 6.626E-34$ Joule seconds

$v=2(9.6E-20)/(6.626E-34)=3.067E14$ cycles per second

wavelength = lambda = c/v where c is the speed of light equal to 3E8 m/s

lambda = $(3E8)/(3.067E14) = 9.78E-7$ meters

1 micrometer = 1E-6 meters

lambda ~ 1 micrometer (This is where the visible spectrum begins)

So we see the visible spectrum for one photon of light begins where the energy is 2 bue. This is an output of 1 "bue". Thus units fall in sync with Nature here as well,

We can see that the mile has further connection to Nature than just the golden ratio, and square root of two over two, which I should point out is the sin of 45 degrees and the cosine of 45 degrees, 45 degrees the angle of maximum distance for the trajectory of a projectile.

We ask: How far is far?

I could say the distance from my house to the village (about a mile) is close. Yet, if I consider the distance from my bedroom to the front door, the distance to the village is far. Everything is relative. Therefore, what can we say is close and what can we say is far? Perhaps the answer to that is embedded in Nature. Let us consider something on the smallest scale we know, the distance of an electron from a proton in an atom of hydrogen and call the distance of one from the other as close. It is about 0.053 nanometers. That is, point zero five three billionths of a meter (0.053E-9 m). Let us consider that which is closest to us on the largest scale we know, the distance to the nearest star, alpha centauri and call it far. It is 4.367 light years away (one ly is 9.56E15 meters) putting alpha cenatauri about 25.6 trillion miles way. We will take the geometric mean of of the electron-proton separation in a hydrogen atom with the earth-alpha centauri separation and consider the result an average manageable distance.

One light year is 9.46E15 meters.

(9.46E15 m/ly)(4.367 ly)=4.13E16 m

sqrt[(0.053E-9 m)(4.13E16 m)]=sqrt(2189526 square meters)=1,480 meters

(1,480 m)(1 km/1000 m) = 1.480 kilometers

(1.480 km)(one mile/1.60934 kilometers)=0.9196 miles ~ 1 mile

Therefore, when humans chose the unit of a mile to measure distance, they may have been in tune with the cosmos (atoms of hydrogen and the closest star).

What We Now Have

We have an energy of 2 bue, where the energy of a photon begins for the visible spectrum of an electronic eye receiving 1 "bue" at one micrometer. We have an acceleration, the acceleration at the surface of the earth connected to kilometers and the circumference of the earth through our integral. We have the unit of a mile, shown to be significant. From these three we can determine a mass:

(1 mile)(1 km/0.621 mi) =161,000 cm

1.92E-12 ergs = 2 bue

1.92E-12 ergs = (161,000 cm)(981cm/s/s)m

m =1.2E-20 grams (The Mystery is in whatever this mass means)

mass of a proton: 1.67 E-27

Suffice to say the real search is in finding energies connected to the bue, basic unit of energy. So, I have written a program for computing energies:

```c
#include <stdio.h>
int main (void)
{
printf("\n");
int n, number;
float mass, distance, acceleration, bue, bue_bio, joules, work=0.00;
float h, v, c, lambda, ergs;
printf("We calculate the energy for 1. work done, or 2. kinetic energy
\n");
printf("How many calculations would you like to make? ");
scanf("%i", &n);
printf("\n");
for (int i=1; i<=n; i++)
{
printf("Would you like the bue (basics units of energy) for: \n");
printf("1. Input of work in centimeters-grams-seconds (dyn), or: \n");
printf("2. Input of work in kilograms-meters-seconds? (Newtons) Or,
\n");
printf("3. Input of kinetic energy in centimeters-grams-seconds, or
\n");
printf("4. Input of kinetic energy in kilograms-meters-seconds: \n");
printf("5. Or simply input an energy in ergs: \n");
scanf("%i", &number);
if (number == 1)
{
printf("What is the mass? ");
scanf("%f", &mass);
printf("What is the acceleration? ");
scanf("%f", &acceleration);
printf("What is the distance? ");
scanf("%f", &distance);
work=mass*acceleration*distance;
printf("\n");
bue = work*((1E-5)/(9.6E-20));
bue_bio = work*((1E-5)/(9.6E-20))*49.8;
joules=work*(1E-5);
printf("That is %.2f ergs\n", work);
printf("Which is %.2f joules\n", joules);
printf("Or, that is %.2f calories\n", work*(1E-5)/4.184);
printf("Or, %.2f E18 eV (electron volts)\n", (work*(1E-5)/
(1.602E-19))/1E18);
printf("basic unit of energy (bue electronic): %.2f E16\n", bue/1E16);
printf("bue biological: %.2f E18", bue_bio/1E18);
printf("\n");
printf("\n");
}
```

```
else if (number==5)
{
printf("bue in ergs: 9.6e-13\n");
printf("How many ergs would you like to consider (1.92e-12)? ");
scanf("%f", &ergs);
h=6.626E-27; //erg-seconds//
v=ergs/h;
c=3E10;
lambda=(c/v);
printf("That is a wavlength of: %.4f meters\n", lambda);
printf("Which is: %.4f micrometers", lambda*1E4);
printf("\n");
}
}
}
```

```
jharvard@appliance (~): cd Dropbox
jharvard@appliance (~/Dropbox): make bue
clang -ggdb3 -O0 -std=c99 -Wall -Werror    bue.c  -lcs50 -lm -o bue
jharvard@appliance (~/Dropbox): ./bue

We calculate the energy for 1. work done, or 2. kinetic energy
How many calculations would you like to make? 1

Would you like the bue (basics units of energy) for:
1. Input of work in centimeters-grams-seconds (dyn), or:
2. Input of work in kilograms-meters-seconds? (Newtons) Or,
3. Input of kinetic energy in centimeters-grams-seconds, or
4. Input of kinetic energy in kilograms-meters-seconds:
5. Or simply input an energy in ergs:
5
bue in ergs: 9.6e-13
How many ergs would you like to consider (1.92e-12)? 1.92e-12
That is a wavlength of: 0.0001 meters
Which is: 1.0353 micrometers
jharvard@appliance (~/Dropbox):
```

jharvard@appliance (~): cd Dropbox
jharvard@appliance (~/Dropbox): ./bue

We calculate the energy for 1. work done, or 2. kinetic energy
How many calculations would you like to make? 3

Would you like the bue (basics units of energy) for:
1. Input of work in centimeters-grams-seconds (dyn), or:
2. Input of work in kilograms-meters-seconds? (Newtons) Or,
3. Input of kinetic energy in centimeters-grams-seconds, or
4. Input of kinetic energy in kilograms-meters-seconds:
5. Or simply input an energy in ergs:
1
What is the mass? 25
What is the acceleration? 981
What is the distance? 150

That is 3678750.00 ergs
Which is 36.79 joules
Or, that is 8.79 calories
Or, 229.63 E18 eV (electron volts)
basic unit of energy (bue electronic): 38320.31 E16
bue biological: 19083.51 E18

Would you like the bue (basics units of energy) for:
1. Input of work in centimeters-grams-seconds (dyn), or:
2. Input of work in kilograms-meters-seconds? (Newtons) Or,
3. Input of kinetic energy in centimeters-grams-seconds, or
4. Input of kinetic energy in kilograms-meters-seconds:
5. Or simply input an energy in ergs:
1
What is the mass? 5
What is the acceleration? 150
What is the distance? 25

That is 18750.00 ergs
Which is 0.19 joules
Or, that is 0.04 calories
Or, 1.17 E18 eV (electron volts)
basic unit of energy (bue electronic): 195.31 E16
bue biological: 97.27 E18

Would you like the bue (basics units of energy) for:
1. Input of work in centimeters-grams-seconds (dyn), or:
2. Input of work in kilograms-meters-seconds? (Newtons) Or,
3. Input of kinetic energy in centimeters-grams-seconds, or
4. Input of kinetic energy in kilograms-meters-seconds:
5. Or simply input an energy in ergs:
5
bue in ergs: 9.6e-13
How many ergs would you like to consider (1.92e-12)? 5
That is a wavlength of: 0.0000 meters
Which is: 0.0000 micrometers
jharvard@appliance (~/Dropbox):

The Author

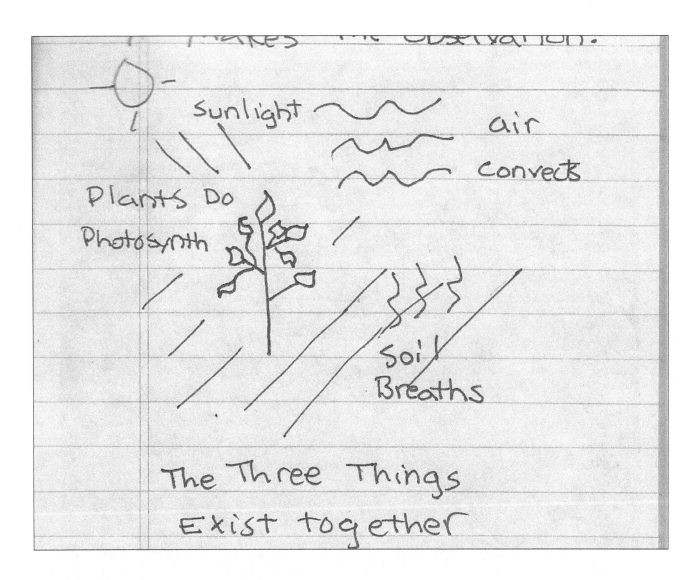

ecotriangle

Prepared for: multiple recipients
Prepared by: Ian Beardsley, Researcher
April 28, 2016
Proposal number: 01

OVNIGITANO

EXECUTIVE SUMMARY

Objective

To establish a connection between soil respiration, photosynthesis by plants, and cooling by convection, as well as the energy received by the sun and chemical energy created by the plants.

Goals

To better understand the operational dynamics of the Earth, so as help it maintain its ability to support life.

Project Outline

For a section of land with its plants and soil types on the order of three meters by three meters:

* Measure cooling of atmosphere by convection.
* Measure oxygen produced by photosynthesis.
* Measure CO_2 respired by soil.
* Measure the amount of chemical energy produced by the plant.
* Measure how much energy the plant/plants received from the Sun.
* Do this experiment for several different biomes so we can establish whether the relationship between convection, respiration, photosynthesis, production of chemical energy, and amount of solar energy received, is a constant relationship from biome to biome.

BUDGET

Setting Up The Experiment

The list below, for equipment to do the experiment, and the prices for it, will be formulated upon further research.

Description	Quantity	Unit Price	Cost
Item 1	55	$ 100	$ 5,500
Item 2	13	$ 90	$ 1,170
Item 3	25	$ 50	$ 1,250
Total			**$ 7,920**

The Earth receives 1,370 Joules of energy per second per square meter. That results in surface temperature increased by greenhouse gases, but cooled by convection. For the planet to not be warming, but to have a constant yearly average temperature, it must be in equilibrium. This means the earth, once it reaches a certain temperature, must lose as much energy as it receives. The earth currently receives more energy than it loses, approximately one watt per square meter, which means the planet is warming.

Convection is the motion of fluids, such as gases, due to expansion from being hotter than the gases above them, by the ideal gas law that relates pressure to temperature and inversely so, to volume. The expansion of gases is a cooling effect. The equation is: $PV = nRT$. R is the ideal gas constant, and n is the number of moles of the substance being considered.

Soil Respiration is the production of CO_2 when organisms in the soil breathe. It includes plant roots, rhizosphere, microbes, and fauna. This is key to providing CO_2 to the atmosphere, which is source of the CO_2 for plants to do photosynthesis, which not only produces the air we breathe, but allows plants to make chemical energy, such as the sugar $C_6H_{12}O_6$, which is at the bottom of the food chain, the ultimate source for food since animals, the source of protein for humans, graze on it.

The UFO Journal Of Ian Beardsley From 2015 To 2016

by

Ian Beardsley

UFO Methodology

By

Ian Beardsley

Copyright © 2016 by Ian Beardsley

If You See A UFO, By All Means, Estimate Its Distance From You

In computer science where we make artificial intelligence based on the way we understand humans function, we have added some things to these robots or AI that humans cannot do, or so they say. I refer to depth perception. The AI scientist put two detectors on AI so that it can use their separation to do parallax calculations for enabling the AI to determine the distance to something. It is commonly referred to as a range finder. The AI scientist believe humans cannot do this. That is if you see a ufo and it looks small, you say it is far away because of that, but in reality it IS small so it could be close up. I disagree and will explain why I think the human mind is a range finder and can estimate the distance to something, that is, I will explain why I think humans have depth perception. Here goes. If we have two eyes, we can use their separation to do parallax, just like a computer does, and indeed estimate the distance to something. In order to do this we have to say the mind understands how far apart your eyes are in order to do a parallax computation. I believe the human mind somewhere deep in its recesses understands the separation of the eyes, can see the object location with one of the eyes, and distinguish it from the view of the object from the other eye, and use that information in a parallax computation that results in the mind doing a reasonable estimate of the distance to the object. That is why I can estimate an airplane is two miles away, and be reasonably correct. I can do this without referring to my understanding of the size of the plane and inferring its distance from this by its decrease in size. I know I can do this, because I can estimate the distance to an airplane at night, when only its lights are shining and I have know way of seeing its size.

UFO Methodology

1. Time: 2:20 AM Jan 8, 2016

2. Location: Los Angeles

   a) from this can find your lattitude

   b) from this can find your longitude

   c) from this can find your time zone

3. coming out of South east
   heading north-west

4. covered 2 miles in on minute
   (about eight city blocks)
   a. from this can determine it's velocity

5.

a = 30ft
b = 30ft
d = unknown
e = unknown

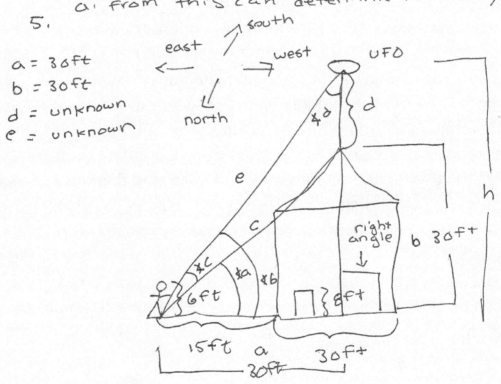

$$c^2 = a^2 + b^2 = 30^2 + 30^2 = 900 + 900 = 1800$$

$$c^2 = 1800 \quad c = \sqrt{1800} = 42.426$$

$$\tan \angle a = \frac{b}{a} = \frac{30}{30} = 1$$

$$\text{arctan } \frac{b}{a} = \text{arctan } 1 = \angle = 45^\circ$$

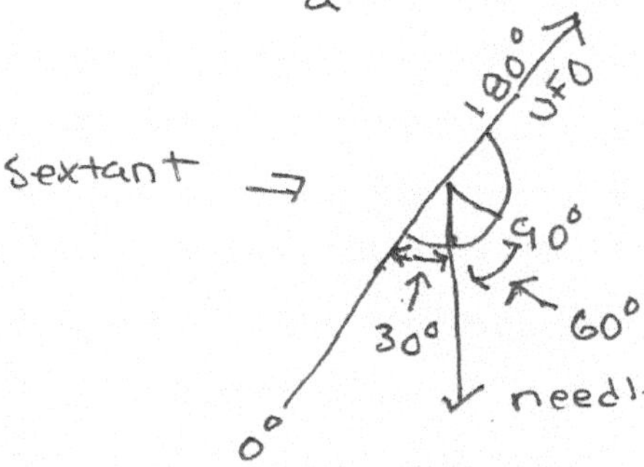

You need a sextant to find ∠b (angle b) ~~altitude~~

Sextant →

needle points to center of earth

$$\tan 60^\circ = \frac{b+d}{a} = \frac{30+d}{30} = \frac{h}{30}$$

$$1.732 = \frac{h}{30} \qquad h = 51.96 \text{ ft}$$
$$= \text{altitude}$$

$$\text{Velocity} = \frac{2 \text{ miles}}{1 \text{ minute}} \cdot \frac{60 \text{ seconds}}{\text{minute}} \cdot \frac{60 \text{ minutes}}{1 \text{ hour}}$$

$$= \frac{2 \text{ miles}}{1 \text{ minute}} \cdot \frac{60 \text{ minutes}}{1 \text{ hour}}$$

$$= 120 \text{ miles an hour}$$

Reading a compass in the
northern hemisphere

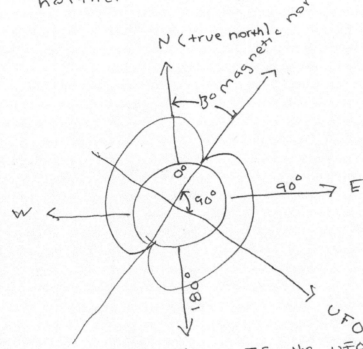

N (true north)   magnetic north

13° magnetic

0°

90°   90°   E

90°

W

180°

S

UFO

The amount of
degrees east of
true north that
is magnetic north
is called Declination.
It varies with your
lattitude and change
from day to day.
Google Declination to
get the Calculator that
Calculates it for your
lattitude, longitude and date.

If the UFO reads
90°, that is 90°
East of magnetic
North. True north
for my lattitude
(Los Angeles) is
13° west of magnetic
north. Therefore you
have to add 13°. The
UFO Pictured here is:
90° + 13° = 103° East

Compass And Sextant

Declination

Date 2015-08-14

Latitude 34° N

Longitude 117° W

Elevation 0.0 km GPS

Model Used WMM2015

Declination 11.93° E changing by

0.09° W per year

Uncertainty 0.33°

Compass shows the approximate bearing of the
magnetic north (MN)

Magnetic declination is the angle between true north and the horizontal trace of the
local magnetic field. In general, the present day field models such as the IGRF and
World Magnetic Model (WMM) are accurate to within 30 minutes of arc for the
declination. However, local anomalies exceeding 10 degrees, although rare, do exist.

Document created: 2015-08-19 03:51 UTC

Help: How to interpret results Questions: geomag.models@noaa.gov

Printout OF Magnetic Declination by Online Calculator

July 09, 2015 I decide to film a chemtrail, but hear a helicopter to the North. I turn my camera to the North and film a black Helicopter heading West:

I then point the camera at the chemtrail. I later take the film in and look at what I have got with my glasses one and it turns out I have a black orb:

The next day, July 10, 2015, I hear a hawk. I go outside with my camera and find it is on a tree limb in the line of sight with where I filmed the black orb due west about 20 to 30 degrees above the horizon. Then suddenly another hawk comes and attacks the first hawk, it leaves the branch and the other one takes its place in that spot for about 15 to 30 second, then leaves:

I report my UFO sighting to MUFFON and it is case number 67958, which I find interesting because it is composed of the integers 5,6,7,8,9.

MUFON Sighting Report

Thank you for your sighting report!

Please note your case number is

67958

As a token of our appreciation, we invite you to
a free subscription to Filer's Files.

Filer's Files is a summary of UFO sightings
and other interesting events from all over the world
brought to you by
George Filer - MUFON Eastern Region Director.

Simply click the button below,
enter your email address in the box provided,
and click submit.

Join Filer's Files List

MUFON Homepage

I have been attempting to measure a repeat of the SETI Wow! Signal with a crude radio telescope I built, which was received on August 15, 1977 at 10:17 PM ET.

Interesting Problems In The Sciences
By Ian Beardsley

Since my sighting was case number 67958. I decide to look up case number 56789. It turns out to be in Utah, June 02, 2014 at 10:17 PM, the same 10:17 PM that SETI detected the Wow! Signal in Sagittarius. I look at a map of Utah and see that the state is surrounded by the UFO hot spots: Wyoming of Devil's Tower where contact was first made in Close Encounters of the Third Kind the movie by Steven Spielberg, Nevada of the secret military base Area 51, where there are believed to be ETs, Arizona where the annual UFO Congress meets, and New Mexico where the famous UFO crash site was in Roswell. But most incredibly, I notice at the center of Utah is a city called Nephi, which is Hebrew for Anunnaki, the Aliens that Zecharia Sitchin says made contact with ancient humans and gave them science and agriculture, who were written about in ancient Sumerian cuneiform:

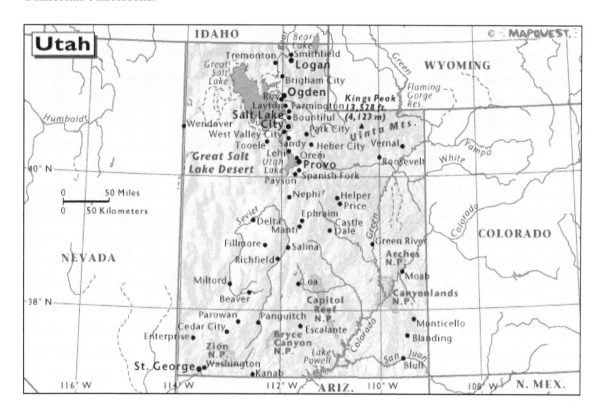

Claremont California, September 14, 2015

A UFO Flying Towards Venus

In film not enhanced: Venus Appears Alone: It is about 5:48 AM, September 14, 2015. This image is at 23 seconds in the video:

About 5 seconds later, something appears that is moving towards Venus. This image is at 33 Seconds:

Here, we pull a clip out of the enhanced footage showing Venus (Right) and The UFO (Left) together. (1 Min 06 Sec)

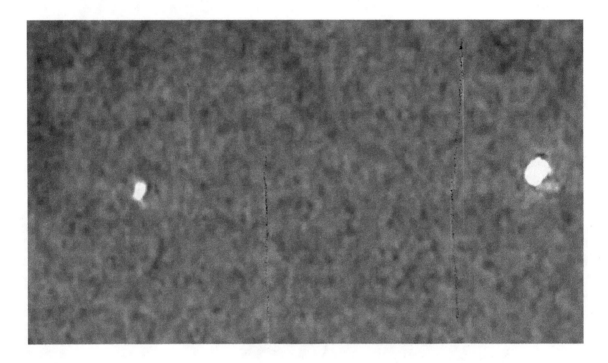

Here we pull out a clip from the enhanced footage of just the UFO (1 Min 12 Sec).

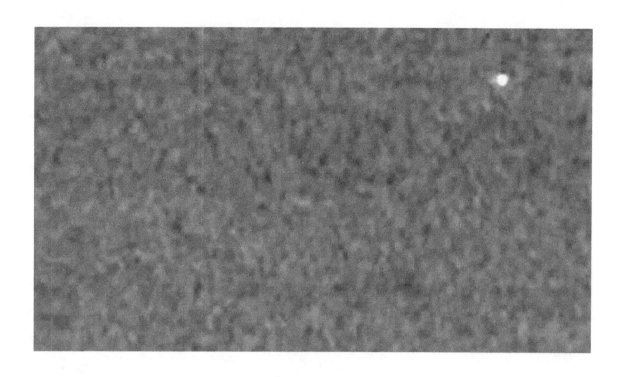

Let us zoom in on that last, enhanced image of just the UFO alone:

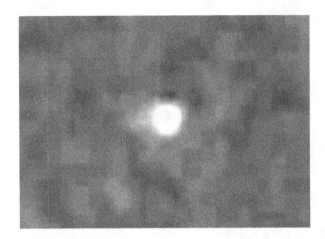

It September 30, 2015 4:30 PM and I have just submitted a UFO report to MUFFON:

MUFON Sighting Report

Thank you for your sighting report!

Please note your case number is

71021

As a token of our appreciation, we invite you to
a free subscription to Filer's Files.

Filer's Files is a summary of UFO sightings
and other interesting events from all over the world
brought to you by
George Filer - MUFON Eastern Region Director.

Simply click the button below,
enter your email address in the box provided,
and click submit.

Join Filer's Files List

MUFON Homepage

Case Number	Date Submitted	Date of Event	Short Description	Location of Event		Long Description	Attachments
				City	State/Country		
71022	2015-09-30	2015-08-25	Heard loud low flying jets, looked up in sky, saw sphere object come from west turn abruptly and go north.	Morgan Hill	CA, US	VIEW	photo92.JPG
71021	2015-09-30	2015-09-14	Filmed Venus 5:48 AM, white speck appeared left to it moving towards it, then disappeared.	Claremont	CA, US	VIEW	VenusUFO091415.mp4
71020	2015-09-30	2015-09-24	ON A THURSDAY NIGHT I WENT TO WALK THE DOGS AT ABOUT 9:20. I LOOKED UP AT THE SKY AND SAW A VERTICAL, STAR COLORED, LINE HOVERING ABOVE THE POWER LINES.	DAWSON	PA, US	VIEW	
71019	2015-09-30	2015-08-14	tic tac shaped blue plasma from rear.	manchester	GB	VIEW	
71018	2015-09-30	2015-09-28	Thought we were watching the clouds pass the "moon" weird night.	Cumberland	MD, US	VIEW	088.jpg 089.jpg 090.jpg 091.jpg 092.jpg 093.jpg 094.jpg 095.jpg 096.jpg 097.jpg
71017	2015-09-30	2015-05-25	My son was recording the storm and caught this what appears to be a UFO in the clouds. We didn't t see it until he was showing another child the pink flourescent lights and then they saw the object before the light beam appeared	Fort Worth	TX, US	VIEW	20150527202115.mp4
71016	2015-09-30	2015-07-25	Bright like an orb and on fire, lit up the sky as it fell.	Austell	GA, US	VIEW	
71015	2015-09-30	2015-08-30	uniboo like obeject kind of wath the german were working on in 2 world war	eastman	QC, CA	VIEW	
71013	2015-09-30	2015-09-26	Driving up Frederick Street towards Old Fritzstown Road observed a Round, White Blinking ORB move across mt Front View . It was Ascending Weirdly towards the Dark Clouds on my Right, It was not a Plane,Helicopter or anything		PA, US	VIEW	

Long Description of Sighting Report

I was filming Venus with a camcorder as it was rising in the East. At 5:48 AM, while filming, an object appeared that did not look like a plane, helicopter, or satellite. It did not move like any of these either. It appeared, while filming, just to the left of Venus, and moving towards it at a slight descent. Then after about 10 second it disappeared before reaching Venus. I have worked in astronomy four four years at the state observatory in Oregon. If I were to compare it to anything, I would have to say it looked more like a natural satellite orbiting jupiter (through a 2.5 inch refractor) than a star. One has to ask: "What is a natural satellite doing appearing, moving towards venus, then disappearing? It looks to me, like light reflected off a metallic surface.

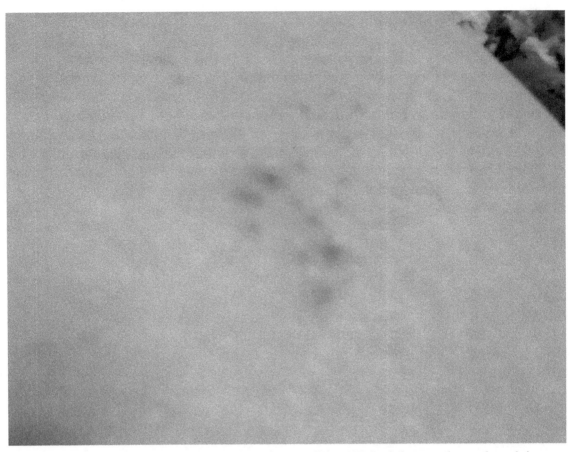

This photo of a mark on my thigh is the same as those UFO abductees have that claim
they are from implants. (Photo taken 12 09 15 at 12:07 AM)

While contemplating extraterrestrial UFOs I make connections like, this pattern in a quilt on my bed with this flex corner vector equilibrium hanging up on my wall:

I find it strange to see a plane flying vertically for such a long period (perhaps a trick plane could briefly) but without an airfoil due to horizontal motion there can be no lift. Vertical flight is more typical of a rocket. This was filmed from Southern California (Claremont) about 40 minutes inland from Los Angeles. I couldn't see it in the camera because of glare, so I had to point the camera best I could at what I was seeing with the naked eye. That is why the plane is not very well centered. This photo comes from a film I took on Dec 17 2015 at about 1:30 PM

Dec 19 9:05PM 2015 there is a search light in the south-west pointing to exactly where I filmed the vertical plane on Dec 17 2015. (Next Page).

The Search For Extraterrestrial Contact On August 14 2015

by

Ian Beardsley

copyright © 2015 by Ian Beardsley

More Entries August 14, 2014

I should probably say I think extraterrestrials sent the Wow signal on August 15, 1977 because the Earth rotates through 15 degrees in on hour: August 15 => 15, 1977 => 7+7+1 = 15 and August => month 8, and 9/5 = 1.8. One takes you around a circle leaving 0.8 and 0.8(360) = 288. 360 - 288 = 72 degrees. 722 is 4(9/5) = 7.2. In 2001: A Space Odyssey the AE35 Antenna is reported to fail within 72 hours. 72 hours is 3 days in that 24(3) = 72 and 0.72 Astronomical Units is the Venus-Earth Separation, Venus a failed Earth. Also, the precession of the earth equinoxes is on degree every 72 years. We also look for ETs on August 14, 14, and 16 2014, 2015, and 2016 because that is a three day period (72 hours) and Carbon, the basis of life is in group 14, Nitrogen is the most abundant element in the Earth's atmosphere and is in group 15, and Oxygen, needed to breathe, is in group 16 (The Periodic Table). Also, these elements make amino acids, the building blocks of life. We see that 72 is of prime importance. The SETI Wow signal lasted 72 seconds.

Had theory predicting ET signal for August 14, 15, 16 of 2015. Was only able to make crude radio telescope. Received signal between 10:00 PM and 10:15 PM August 14 2015. Need to analyze duration of signal and time between them to determine whether there is a mathematical pattern indicating intelligence.

The Radio Telescope is a 10 year old Direct TV Reception dish given to me by my brother. Power source is 12 volt AC to DC Adapter. Used $1.75 satellite finder for meter to measure strength of radio signals. Set gain at noise level, anything on top of that will make it sound.

Signal meter reading the hypothesized ET signal at 6. Reads five with no ET signal (5 is background noise.)

The Compass and Sextant Used

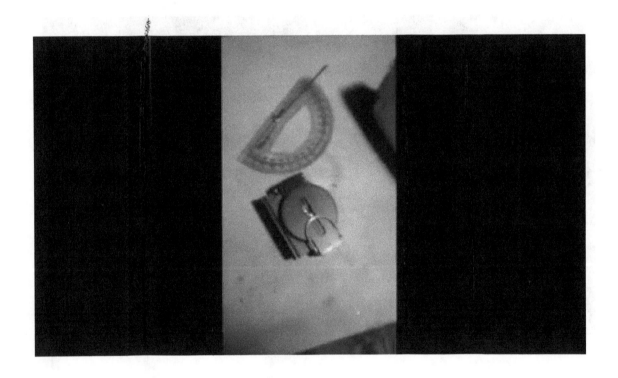

Had theory predicting ET signal for August 14, 15, 16 of 2015. Was only able to make crude radio telescope. Received signal between 10:00 PM and 10:15 PM August 14 2015. Need to analyze duration of signal and time between them to determine whether there is a mathematical pattern indicating intelligence.

The signals were around Sagittarius and Aquila on Aug 14 (as predicted), precisely +30 Degrees altitude, and 153 degrees South East at 10:00 to 10:15. They came in 4 four bursts of one, three, four, three approximately 84 seconds apart.

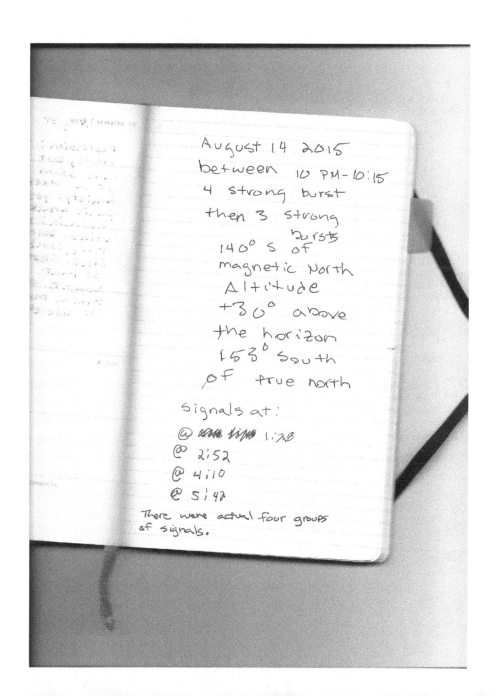

```
1:30 - 1:35        90 - 95        seconds
2:55               175.           5
2:56               176            0 → 1/10
3:01               181            0 → 5/10
4:12 - 4:13        252 - 253      0 → 1/10
4:15 - 4:19        255 - 259      1
4:27 - 4:31        267 - 271      4
4:33 - 4:48        273 - 288      4
5:43 - 5:44        343 - 344      15
6:14 - 6:24        374 - 384      1
6:29 - 6:33        389 - 393      10
                                  4
```

signal

```
0                                        signal
1   0                     0                O
2   85 ////////////       85
3                         176 - 90 = 86  } 85
4   5                     181 - 90 = = 91
5   252 - 81 = 171        252 - 96 = 162
6   255 - 252 = 3         255 - 90 = 165
7   267 - 255 = 12        267 - 90 = 177  } 162
8                         273 # 96 = 183
                          343 - 90 = 253
    91 + 77 + 85          374 - 90 = 284  } 253
    ─────────── = 84.3    389 - 90 = 299
        3
```

```
253 - 162 = 91  burst 4   (3 signals)
162 - 85 = 77   burst 3   (4 signals)
85 - 0 = 85     burst 2   (3 signals)
0 - 0 = 0       burst 1   (1 signal)

253/3 = 84 1/3
```

August 14 2015 10:00 PM - 10:15PM

seconds	bursts			
0	1			
85	3			
162	4			
253	3			

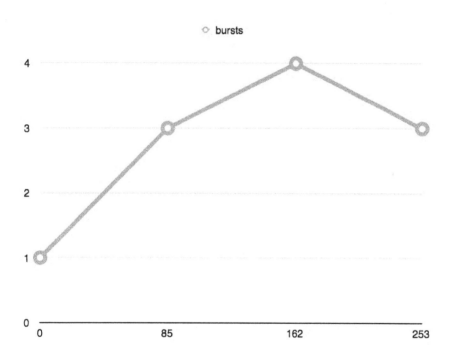

bursts

Table 1

signal	duration
0	5
1	0.10
2	0.01
3	0.01
4	1
5	4
6	4
7	15
8	1
9	10
10	4

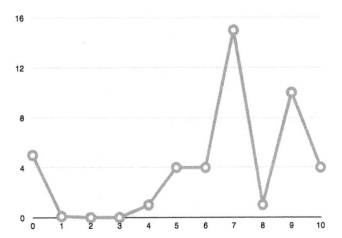

Table 1

signal	seconds
0	175
1	176
2	181
3	252
4	255
5	267
6	273
7	343
8	374
9	389

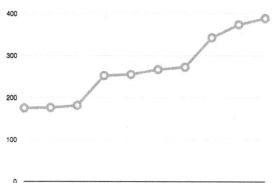

seconds

seconds

39

Duration Of Each Burst

Burst	Seconds
0	0
1	5
2	6
3	36
4	50

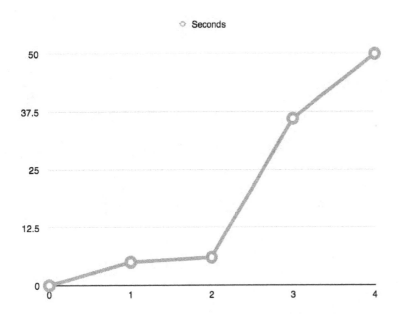

◇ Seconds

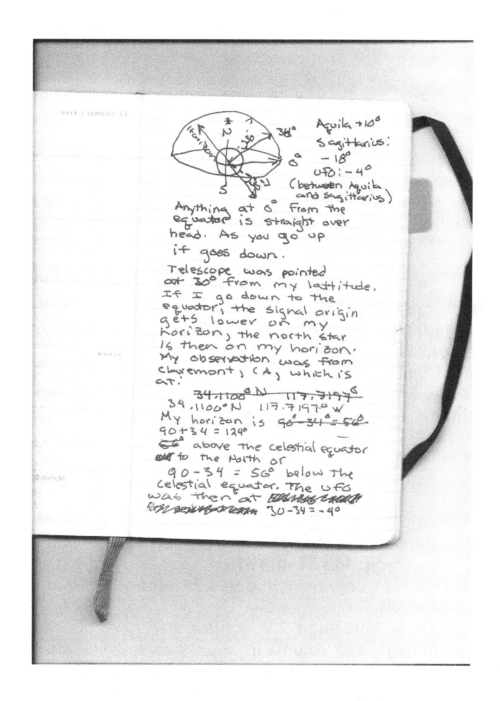

Aguila +10°

Sagittarius:
— 18°

UFO: —4°
(between Aguila
and sagittarius)

Anything at 0° From the
equator is straight over
head. As you go up
it goes down.

Telescope was pointed
at 30° From my lattitude.
IF I go down to the
equator, the signal origin
gets lower on my
horizon, the north star
Is then on my horizon.
My observation was From
Claremont, CA, which is
at:

~~34.1100°N 117.7197°~~
34.1100°N 117.7197° W
My horizon is ~~90—34° = 56°~~
90+34 = 124°
~~56°~~ above the celestial equator
~~with~~ to the North or
90—34 = 56° below the
celestial equator. The UFO
was then at ~~xxxxxxxxxx~~
~~xxxxxxxxxx~~ 30—34 = —4°

41

I was filming when I was receiving the hypothetical ET signal. The event being filmed, I was able to measure the duration of the signals and time between them by using the time indicator on the quicktime movie.

UFO RA and Dec (As you can see I put in the wrong time in military time)

Turns out it is much more difficult than I thought to convert degrees above my horizon and azimuth (degrees from true north) to Right Ascension and Declination, but is easy in the sense that there is an online calculator. Here are the results.

Input

Date: August 14 2015
Time: 14:00:00 (10PM PST)
Time Zone Offset: 8 hours west of Greenwich
Daylight Savings Time: add one hour
Lattitude: 34 degrees 00 minutes 00 seconds North
Longitude: 118 degrees 00 minutes 00 seconds West
Epoch Year: 2015

Output:

Local Sidereal Time: 12:51:58
Right Ascension: 14h 31 min 41s
Declination: -21 degrees 6 minutes 26 seconds
Tirion Page: 21
Uranometeria 2000 page: 332 volume ii
Millenium page: 863 volume ii
Clearly whether or not it is daylight savings has little affect on the calculation. The UFO was at about 14 hours 30 min hours 23 right ascension and -21 degrees declination. But none the less the add one hour is correct, it is summer and fall fall back, spring spring forward.

The Wow signal was measured on August 15, 1977 at 10:17 PM Eastern Time. I measured my signal on August 14, 2015 between 10:00 PM and 10:15 PM PST. Measuring the Azimuth with a compass and altitude with a sextant, I was able to use an online converter to get the field of view of the telescope at the time of the signal, which, using Cartes Du Ciel, I was able to obtain maps of the field of view, which were around Libra, Ophiuchus, and Sagittarius. When I worked at the state observatory in Oregon, about 30 years ago, the professor that ran the observatory took me out one night at sunrise to show me his favorite constellation, which was rising with the sun, and it was Ophiuchus. Libra is home to the most likely extrasolar planet to have life (gliese 581) Here is the field of view of the hypothetical ET signal:

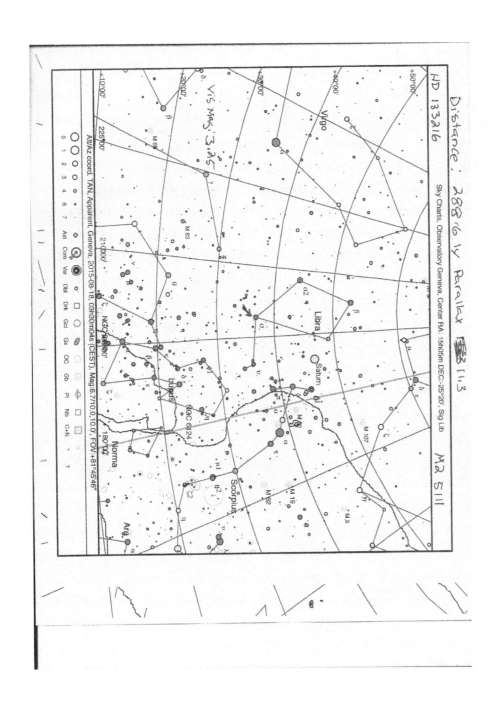

Distance: 288 r6 ly Parallax 隆3 [1.3

HD 133216

Sky Charts, Observatory Geneva, Center RA: 15h05m DEC: -25°20', Sig Lib

M2 5 III

Vis. Mag.: 3.25

Virgo

Libra

Saturn

Lupus

NGC 6124

NGC 5822

Norma

Scorpius

Ara.

Alt/Az coord. TAN, Apparent, Geneva, 2015-08-18, 03h30m04s (CEST), Mag:6.7/10.0,10.0, FOV:+81°45'46"

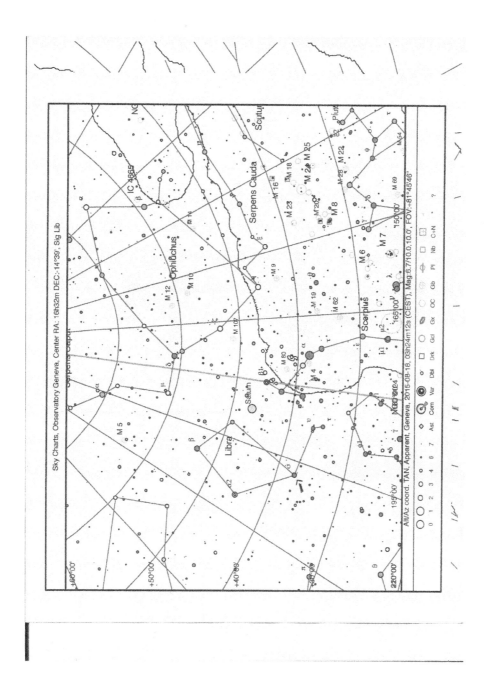

Declination

Date	2015-08-14
Latitude	34° N
Longitude	117° W
Elevation	0.0 km GPS
Model Used	WMM2015
Declination	11.93° E changing by
	0.09° W per year
Uncertainty	0.33°

Compass shows the approximate bearing of the
magnetic north (MN)

Magnetic declination is the angle between true north and the horizontal trace of the
local magnetic field. In general, the present day field models such as the IGRF and
World Magnetic Model (WMM) are accurate to within 30 minutes of arc for the
declination. However, local anomalies exceeding 10 degrees, although rare, do exist.

Document created: 2015-08-19 03:51 UTC

Help: How to interpret results Questions: geomag.models@noaa.gov

The Warm Room

Here are the results with the correct time in military time (They make sense completely):

Input

Date: August 14 2015
Time: 22:00:00 (10PM PST)
Time Zone Offset: 8 hours west of Greenwich
Daylight Savings Time: add one hour
Lattitude: 34 degrees 00 minutes 00 seconds North
Longitude: 118 degrees 00 minutes 00 seconds West
Epoch Year: 2015
Altitude: 30 Degrees
Azimuth: 152 Degrees

Output:

Local Sidereal Time: 20:41:48

Right Ascension: 22h 24 min 33s
Declination: -20 degrees 45 minutes 8 seconds

Tirion Page: 23
Uranometeria 2000 page: 347 volume ii
Millenium page: 1355 volume iii

As you can see the result is about 3 hours east of Sagittarius. This makes sense. I pointed the telescope at the Sagittarius/ Aquila area because that is where my theory predicted the ET signal should come from. But I decided to do a sweep of the sky and when I went a little east of the Sagittarius/Aquila area I got a strong reading and decided to measure over there, because it is still close to the right area. You will find if you look for this position on a sky map, the location of the hypothetical ETs is in the constellation Aquarius, around a planetary nebula there called NGC 7293. I will provide a map of that area that I obtained from Cartes Du Ciel:

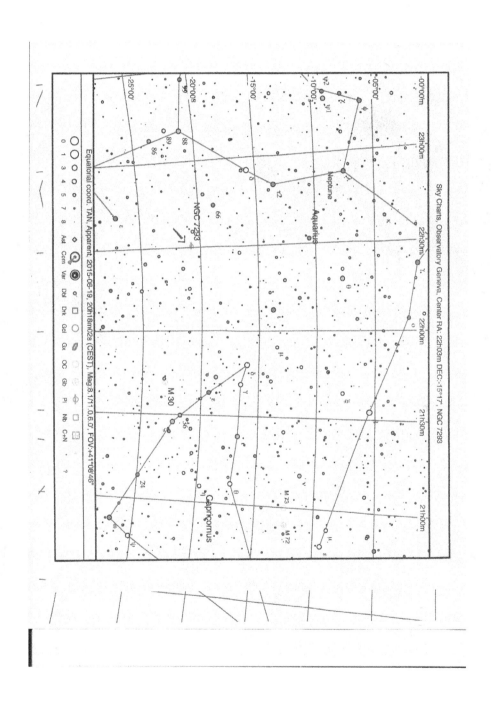

Sky Charts, Observatory Geneva, Center RA: 22h03m DEC: -15°17', NGC 7293

Equatorial coord. TAN, Apparent, 2015-08-19, 20h18m02s (CEST), Mag:8.1/11.0,6.0'; FOV: 41°08'46"

NGC 7296

The Author